AF506146
HERKIMER COUNTY COMMUNITY COLLEGE

Columbia University

Contributions to Education

Teachers College Series

No. 960

AMS PRESS
NEW YORK

Problems and Emotional Difficulties of Negro Children

AS STUDIED IN SELECTED COMMUNITIES
AND ATTRIBUTED BY PARENTS AND CHILDREN
TO THE FACT THAT THEY ARE NEGRO

By REGINA MARY GOFF, Ph.D.

*Teachers College, Columbia University
Contributions to Education, No. 960*

BUREAU OF PUBLICATIONS
TEACHERS COLLEGE, COLUMBIA UNIVERSITY
NEW YORK, 1949

Library of Congress Cataloging in Publication Data

Goff, Regina Mary.
    Problems and emotional difficulties of Negro children.

    Reprint of the 1949 ed., issued in series: Columbia
University. Teachers College. Contributions to educa-
tion, no. 960.
    Originally presented as the author's thesis, Columbia.
    Bibliography: p.
    1. Negro children. 2. Child study. 3. Negroes--
Psychology. I. Title. II. Series: Columbia Univer-
sity. Teachers College. Contributions to education,
no. 960.
E185.86.G6 1972   155.9'2   76-176808
ISBN 0-404-55960-3

From the edition of 1949, New York
First AMS edition published in 1972
Manufactured in the United States

AMS PRESS, INC.
NEW YORK, N. Y.   10003

ACKNOWLEDGMENTS

The writer is deeply grateful to Professor Arthur T. Jersild, who served as sponsor of the study, for his stimulating guidance, interest, and encouragement throughout all stages of the work. For invaluable criticisms and suggestions, she is also indebted to Professors Irving Lorge, Goodwin Watson, and Otto Klineberg, all of whom generously served as committee members.

For permission and help in securing names and addresses of children and parents from community and recreation centers, the writer wishes to thank Dr. Sophie Robison, Miss Jennie Wahlert, Mrs. Ethel Murray, Mrs. Anna Lee Scott, and Mr. James A. Cook. To the children and parents who so graciously cooperated, she wishes to express sincere appreciation.

For grants making possible the pursuance and completion of the study, great indebtedness is felt toward the General Education Board.

The writer is also extremely grateful to her parents for their enthusiastic encouragement and spiritual guidance.

R. M. G.

CONTENTS

Problems and Emotional Difficulties of Negro Children

Chapter One

INTRODUCTION

THIS STUDY is an investigation of the problems, fears, annoyances, frustrations, and other emotional difficulties that Negro children experience, according to their own reports, by reason of the fact that they are Negro. The study does not attempt to deal with underlying motivations, but with the manifest difficulties or annoyances as they appear to children, and which might be thought of as environmental or social pressures. A further aspect of the study is an exploration of the nature of the guidance provided by parents, according to their own reports, in dealing with these problems, and a study of the effectiveness of such guidance as judged by children and parents.

The specific problems proposed may be stated as follows:

1. What are the emotional difficulties which Negro children have because of their group identity? This problem raises an additional question: Do these difficulties vary in terms of factors such as geographical section, socio-economic level, sex, and skin color?

2. What inner feelings are associated with these problems? This problem also raises the question whether these inner feelings vary in relation to factors such as geographical section, socio-economic level, and sex.

3. What impulses are directed toward the environment?

4. What types of responses are made to these difficulties?

5. According to the reports of children, are the overt responses indicative of what they felt like doing?

6. What forms of guidance do parents give? This problem raises the same question presented in problem 1.

7. Is the guidance given by parents effective, as judged by children?

8. Which social difficulties appear to produce the greatest effect on personality development?

The study attempts to discover specific social pressures which create problems for the Negro child, and to isolate these difficulties in the hope that survival techniques or satisfying adjustment mechanisms may be developed to offset their effects on personality development. It also attempts to discover forms of guidance or strategic philosophies of parents which may prove effective in adjustment problems.

THE PROCEDURE

The interview method was used in the study. When this method was chosen it was with the understanding that questions carefully prepared in advance could be revised and improved through preliminary tryouts. It was also understood that the material would be used both quantitatively and qualitatively. The limitations of the method, however, are important considerations in ascertaining the validity of results. The question arises, are the reports given by interviewees true accounts of experiences? This will be discussed later in considering the results obtained. In addition, it should be pointed out that in an interview study there is the possibility of a personal element entering the picture. The fact that a little time must elapse between the moment when the people speak and the moment when the material is written down suggests that a certain amount of selection of material must take place in the interviewer's mind. Recognition of this factor caused the investigator to attempt full recording of interviews as quickly and accurately as possible. In addition, attention was given to dress, speech patterns, general manner, and other observable features about the interviewer which it was felt might make for better rapport, and subsequently encourage freedom and honesty of response.

The final interview form was standardized on the basis of reports obtained during a two-month exploratory period of free discussion, designed to discover the kinds of questions that could best elicit the desired information. When the final form was completed, systematic entries were made and responses recorded verbatim, insofar as possible, on prepared blanks. Notations were also made of lack of response to questions. As little as possible was written in the presence of the interviewee. Usually, a significant word would serve to recall a whole line of thought, and complete reports were written as soon after the interview as possible.

Each of the 150 children in the study was asked by a Negro investigator to give an account of the kinds of unpleasant experiences he had had with white children or white adults; to tell how he felt when the experience occurred; to tell what he felt like doing; to describe what he actually did; to recall the guidance given by his mother; and to comment on the effectiveness of the guidance.

Each of the 150 mothers in the study was asked to recall any experiences with white children or white adults which their children had reported to them as unpleasant; to tell the kind of guidance given; and to speak of the helpfulness of the guidance. Parents were also asked to express their opinions on segregation, interracial meetings, and the effectiveness of churches in intergroup betterment, and to say what they believed would help most in fostering better relationships.

The approach in the interview process was always friendly and informal. An early attempt was made to establish a relationship which would suggest that the child was a helper, and to indicate that there was no intention of finding fault with him. Sometimes as much as ten minutes was spent in this initial period. After preliminaries, the child was asked to verify his name, age, and address. An effort was then made to introduce questions bearing on his relations with white children and adults. This was done at first, insofar as possible, in general terms, without the use of leading or direct questions. However, the interview was so planned that if the child did not himself volunteer information on the subject, he was asked a few direct questions about it.

The investigator tried not to follow a rigid or mechanical interview procedure. As a matter of fact, children varied so much in the way they responded that it would not have been possible in any event to make interviews exactly identical. There were, however, a number of major points which each interview was designed to cover.

In the first question or series of questions, the child was asked to tell whom he played or sat with at school or regarded as his friends. After he had identified such persons he was asked to say what it was he liked about them, and what they looked like. The aim here was to get the child to indicate whether the persons he felt friendly with were white or colored.

Another series bore on the topic of quarrels, fights, and misunderstandings. Here again the general reference to "other children" was made before any specific question was raised about bad relations with white children as distinguished from those with other groups. Among the questions in this series were: Do you ever have quarrels or fights with other children? Are there some children who seem to want to fight more than others? Which children are they? Are these colored children or white children, or are they both white and colored? Do some children at your school do things which you do not like? What do they do? Tell me what happens. Are these things ever done by white children? When this happened [specific item mentioned], how did you feel? What did you feel like doing? What did you do? Did it work? Did you tell your mother? What did she say? Did you do it? Did it work? Do colored children do these things too? How do you feel? What do you do?

The next series of questions was designed to cover the general theme of ridicule and being made fun of, as distinguished from actual fighting and person-to-person conflict. Included in the questions in this series were: Have white children ever made fun of you? What did they say? When this happened how did you feel? What did you feel like doing? What did you do? Did you tell your mother? What did she say? Did it work? Do colored children do these things too? How did you feel? What did you do?

A general comment in relation to the teacher * was designed to find out whether the behavior of the white teacher reflected an attitude interpreted by the child as meaning that she had a low opinion of the child. Children were asked: Do you have a white teacher or a colored teacher? Is she nice to you? Is she nice to the class? Does she like colored children? Why do you say what you do? Whom does she like best in the class? Is this a colored child? What do you want to be when you grow up? Have you

* Questions concerning teachers and school activities were presented to New York children only.

told your teacher about it? What does she say about it? Do you think that she would like for you to become a lawyer, a doctor, or a teacher? Does your room ever have class plays, entertainments, or programs? Have you ever taken part in one? Tell me about the part which you had. How did you come to get it? Did you choose it? How did you feel about the part? Did you like it? (If not, what did you do about it? What did your mother say about it?) Does the class ever take trips away from the school? Do you have a good time with the white children on the trip?

Another series of questions dealt with relations with tradespeople in the community at large. These questions were presented in somewhat the following manner: Do you ever have trouble with the grocer, butcher, bakery man, or candy store man? Tell me about it. Do you ever have to wait long in order to be served? Why do you think this happens? How do you feel when these things happen? What do you do? What does your mother say you should do?

Somewhat akin to the above group were questions relating to activities in the wider community: Have you ever been turned away from a park, playground, museum, or any place where other people go? What happened? How did you feel? What did you feel like doing? What did you do? Did you tell your mother? What did she say?

Questions about attitudes toward stereotyped Negro characterizations were also presented. These included the following: Do you go to the movies? What do you think about movies with Negro characters? Do you like them? Do you listen to the radio? What do you think about Negro radio characters? Do you like them?

In order that types of experiences not otherwise mentioned might be discovered, children were asked: Have you ever gone into a white neighborhood? How did you feel? What happened?

Concerning sources of guidance other than the home, children were asked: Do you go to Sunday school? Does your Sunday school teacher say anything to you about getting along with white people? What does she say?

In order to save time in interviews with parents, and to reveal without stalling what parents would soon realize anyhow, interviewers came directly to the point so that parents knew they were seeking information concerning Negro–white relations. After the usual identifying information had been obtained, parents were asked to relate any experiences their children had reported to them which involved white children or white adults, to explain how they handled the situation, and to state whether they thought the suggestions given were helpful.

The investigator soon found, however, that parents were generally vague about facts concerning children's relationships. Since this is a study designed as much to probe into attitudes—the ways people feel—as to give an inventory of established facts, the opportunity was taken to part from straight facts and to raise hypothetical questions, or questions that involved opinions and feelings rather than specific difficulties which children reported. Parents were therefore asked the following questions: What is the best advice to give your child if he is called Nigger, Sambo, Snowball, or any other such name? What should he do if white children start a fight with him? What should he do if he is turned away from a park, playground, museum, theatre, or any place where other people go?

Relative to their own contacts and activities with white persons, parents were asked: Do you have any white friends? Do you exchange visits? Do you belong to any interracial groups? Do you get help from them? What good do you think they serve? Do you think white people are justified in demanding segregation?

Further comments were sought relative to the influence of the church. Parents were asked: What is your minister's attitude on Negro–white relations? What does he tell you to do when racial situations arise? Is he a fair-minded person? Do you think of him as a peacemaker?

Finally, parents were asked to discuss their views of what would help most in bettering Negro–white relations.

During the interviews, special attention was paid to the skin color of mothers in order later to try to establish the relationship of skin color to type of guidance given.

The interviewer was careful to see that each child was asked the same questions. It was not always necessary, however, to ask each child all of the more detailed questions, since some children elaborated on experiences with little or no encouragement. Others were somewhat shy at first, but spoke more freely as the interview progressed, often responding to such comments, made in unhurried fashion, as "That's very interesting. Would you like to tell me more about it?" Care was taken to see that no question suggested an answer.

The investigator was unsuccessful in gaining admittance to schools in both New York and St. Louis because, evidently, of the nature of the problem. Children were therefore sought in their homes, in the Y.M.C.A. and Y.W.C.A., and in Sunday school and Scout groups. Interviews were conducted individually. Complete privacy was not always possible, however. In the case of children in lower income groups in New York, interviews often had to take place on doorsteps and street benches because children were locked out of the house and told to remain out until their mothers returned from work. Children in upper income groups were protectively housed, but, as will be brought out later, their mothers often appeared reluctant to leave them for free participation in the discussion. In St. Louis, children were sought more often in club or organizational settings, and adult interference was thus avoided.

In the lower income group in New York, parents and children were matched. That is, parents whose children had been interviewed were themselves interviewed. However, it soon became apparent that there was no particular relationship between the reports of children and those of parents. That is, parents did not always report the same experiences which children reported. Evidently, what remained with each individual was dependent on its unique meaning for him and on the impression it had made. It was also true that a great many children did not report all such experiences to their parents. Apart from this, the work of locating the parents of particular children was in many instances extremely time-consuming. Homes were seldom provided with telephones, and in many instances three or four trips to a single house were necessary to find parents at home. Since the overlap, or common elements in reports of children and their parents, proved so slight, the idea of matching parents and children was later abandoned as a matter of expediency. In the other groups studied, parents of children who had been interviewed were interviewed if they were available. Otherwise, different parents were sought, from other sources.

The interviews took place from January to July, 1946.

THE SUBJECTS AND THE SETTING

Of the 150 children in the study, 90 lived in New York City and 60 in St. Louis, Missouri.

Missouri, commonly known as a borderline state because it is on the Mason–Dixon line, is nevertheless variously defined. Odum [1] refers to it as Middle Western. Considered with the school segregation law as a criterion, it is Southern. It was a slave state in 1860, and now has laws prohibiting intermarriage. Separation on streetcars and railways is not practiced; but separate eating, entertainment, and church facilities prevail. Restrictive measures based on tradition, reflective of a complex of thought patterns, have molded attitudes which have persisted through time. Negroes in New York, in its Northern setting, have been free of such legal restraints.

The exploration of difficulties with reference to locality has implications which are of cultural significance. Geographical spacing provides opportunities for observing action patterns reflective of attitudes of a cohesive, regional society. In this study, two contrasting societal frameworks are represented.

Children from families of contrasting socio-economic levels were selected because it is generally believed that individuals in different social and economic groups have subjective intellectual and emotional reactions which result in a contrast in thought, feeling, and action. Class patterns, then, which reflect varying degrees of acculturation, which is in turn related to economic status, show observable differences of possible significance in understanding the area of human relationship under investigation. In this study the terms "lower income group" and "upper income group" are used. In addition to occupation, the cultural background of each family was investigated as fully as possible.

[1] Howard Odum, *American Regionalism.* New York, Henry Holt and Company, 1938.

Included in the lower income group were unskilled factory employees, domestic workers, and persons on temporary or permanent relief. Generally, these homes were crowded, poorly furnished, and reflective of low living standards. Books, periodicals, and newspapers were conspicuously absent—one indication of limited educational background. Most of these families were migrants from Southern areas where educational opportunities were, no doubt, rare.

This group, however, cannot be described as homogeneous, for variation in some particulars was noted. Even with uncertain income and spasmodic employment, parents who had an interest in education for their children outnumbered those who preferred early work experience for them. There were also more parents who showed a respect for morals and law and order. The majority of families included in this sample might be thought of as representing the upper and middle levels of the Negro lower income group. A conspicuous commonplace, however, was family disorganization: fathers were usually not members in the home.

The upper income group included those individuals who had steady employment in occupations requiring some training, skill, or professional education—occupations generally considered "white collar" or "respectable." In addition, some were descendants of families referred to as "pioneers" or "old families," and some were members of exclusive clubs. In this group were property owners and community leaders. More numerous, however, were those who had had higher educational experience and good employment than those who could mention family background or any measure of accumulated material goods.

The majority of individuals in this group would probably represent the middle level of the upper income group. Family organization, church membership, education, and refinement were emphasized by all, regardless of their particular rank within the group.

It might be mentioned that "upper class" within the Negro group would probably approximate upper-middle class within the white group.

Low income families in New York, located through records obtained from the after-school recreational center at P.S. 10, 117th and St. Nicholas Avenue, lived in the area from Morningside

Avenue on the west to Fifth Avenue on the east, and from 113th Street on the south to 120th Street on the north. Upper income families in New York were scattered, but generally found north of 135th Street and west of Edgecomb Avenue and Convent Avenue.

Low income families in St. Louis were located through the Y.M.C.A., Carr Square Village Community Center, and Neighborhood House Community Center. They lived in a district bounded by Franklin Avenue on the south, Biddle Street on the north, 19th Street on the west, and 14th Street on the east. This section, according to findings of the Social Planning Council of St. Louis, is part of the city's "decaying core," with a highly concentrated Negro population, and, with the exception of one government housing project, slum conditions.

It should be mentioned that inasmuch as names of children in low income groups in both New York and St. Louis were obtained from lists furnished by community agencies such as recreation centers, it is quite possible that a bias might exist within the sample. That is, children who attend these settings may not be the more aggressive members of the groups, and behavior recorded from their reports may not be typical of the low income group as a whole.

Upper income families in St. Louis were located in the west and northwest sections of the city in the vicinity bounded by Enright Avenue on the south, St. Louis Avenue on the north, Grand Avenue on the east, and Kingshighway on the west. In this area there is a concentration of Negro professional workers, including teachers, clergymen, physicians, and lawyers.[2]

The interviewer was familiar enough with the Negro professional and upper income group in St. Louis to make a fairly accurate selection of interviewees on the basis of the criteria already mentioned. In New York, lack of familiarity with individuals in this group necessitated relying on membership lists of exclusive clubs, which included only families in the upper income group. Although the sampling in the two cities was not achieved in exactly the same way, in the judgment of the investigator there is the possibility that they are equivalent.

[2] Based on analysis presented by Social Planning Council of St. Louis.

TABLE I
Occupations of Low Income Parents

Occupation	NEW YORK		ST. LOUIS	
	Number (60)	*Per Cent*	*Number* (30)	*Per Cent*
Domestic and laundry service	37	62	18	60
Hotel cleaners	7	12	8	27
Unskilled garment workers	11	18	0	0
Unemployed	5	8	4	13

Table I presents the kinds and distribution of occupations of mothers in the low income group in St. Louis and New York. It was necessary to consider maternal occupations because in the larger percentage of low income homes the mother was the sole support.

TABLE II
Occupations of Upper Income Parents

Occupation	NEW YORK		ST. LOUIS	
	Number (30)	*Per Cent*	*Number* (30)	*Per Cent*
Community center directors	2	7	0	0
Social service workers	2	7	2	7
Lawyers	3	10	2	7
Doctors	7	23	4	13
Teachers	0	0	10	33
Chemists	1	3	0	0
Businessmen	3	10	5	17
Government and city employees ..	12	40	7	23

Table II presents the kinds and distribution of occupations of upper income fathers in New York and St. Louis. The occupations of fathers were considered at this level because the fathers in the upper income group assumed support of the family.

TREATMENT OF THE DATA

The children's reports of difficulties were set down on large sheets of paper, and next to each difficulty were placed, in the order indicated, the child's statements of (1) how he felt, (2) what he felt like doing, (3) what he actually did, (4) what his mother told him to do, and (5) his appraisal of the effectiveness of the guidance. This compilation embraced all the responses made by all the children to questions asked, set down in systematic order but without regard to a particular pattern or organization.

The raw data thus transcribed were examined for common elements or similar items that might be placed in the same category. A tentative set of categories representing the difficulties the children had encountered was devised. These categories were then used in analyzing individual records. To check and supplement the efforts of the original worker, two other persons were asked to work independently and to classify the difficulties in terms of the categories. One person was a newspaper woman and instructor in journalism, the other a housewife. Twenty of the interviews were used for this purpose.

After classifications were completed, comparisons were made to see the extent to which the three persons agreed in their analysis of the data in terms of the categories.

The kinds of difficulties reported by the children were evidently of a simple and well-defined character, for disagreement between independent workers at the outset in their analysis of the data was slight. However, when such disagreements occurred, categories were reconsidered. The main problem was that of making the groupings more inclusive. The spread of difficulties under the original categories was so great that the items in some categories were too few. The categories were combined to eliminate overlapping, to eliminate the thin spread of items, and at the same time to achieve accuracy in designating the kind of difficulties reported. For example, rude treatment, insulting behavior, attempt to dominate, and intrusion when not invited—all separate categories originally—were combined under the general heading of rude treatment. Discrimination, segregation, and lack of being accepted on basis of equality as another human being—other forms of behavior judged unfair and suspicious—were combined under the general heading of discrimination. Name-calling and disparaging or belittling statements were combined in the category of ridicule. After reconsideration and refinement of the categories the three workers again classified the data from original records. Out of the 182 difficulties reported, there were but three instances of disagreement.

CATEGORIES USED IN ANALYZING THE DATA

A statement of the categories under which the children's replies were classified, with illustrations of these, follows. The categories are arranged from those representing overt verbal and physical manifestations to those representing more subtle levels.

Overt manifestations

Direct ridicule, including name-calling, disparaging or belittling statements referring to unfavorable qualities alleged to be characteristic of Negroes, and statements implying that the Negro has physical and social traits which attest to inherent weaknesses or differentiate him from white persons:

"The boys told me I didn't belong up there by the river. They said, 'Hey, nigger, don't you know your kind ain't got no business up here!' "

"White boys cuss me and call me ole black nigger. One of them called me a black bitch."

"A woman in the park said, 'It's a pity white people have to mix with niggers. They ought to be separate from them.' "

"The conductor on the trolley called me nigger."

"The teacher said, 'You act just like a darky on the stage, but when somebody talks about your race you don't like it.' "

"Once we went to the museum with the teacher, and when we went to the washroom to wash our hands we met some white children. They started calling us names like nigger children and darky children. Our teacher wasn't with us, and the teacher with the white children didn't scold her class, but she told the Negro children they should have better manners."

"One day the teacher told us she wouldn't take us on no trips because it would be a disgrace to be seen on the street with a bunch of monkeys and laughing hyenas. She said, 'What would my friends say!' "

"I was shining shoes and a white woman stopped me and said, 'Do my shoes need a shine?' I said, 'Yes mam.' She said, 'You little black nigger. I ought to knock your teeth out for insulting me.' "

These statements would seem to indicate consciously designed verbal attacks which aim to stigmatize, label, or belittle; and inherent in them are attitudes which imply rejection. Beyond this, it might be stated that those who tend to derogate others indicate their own feelings of inadequacy and inferiority.[3]

Physical ill-treatment, including threats of violence by white persons:

"When we left the museum, we went to the Automat to eat. I went to get a glass of water and this white woman slapped me in the face."

"A white man on Riverside Drive was crossing the street with his dog, and I almost ran into them. He knocked me off my bicycle."

"The store man on the corner doesn't like colored people. One day I went to take a bottle back, and when I asked him for the nickel he snatched the bottle and wouldn't give it to me. Then he pushed me out of the door."

"Once we were playing outside in front of a store and the white man came out and threw water on us and started chasing us."

"I went to get on the street car, and a white man jerked me off, and let a white woman on and then he got on."

"I went to the Police Circus and sat down by some white people. The white man reached over and pinched me real hard."

"I went in a store to sell some Sunday papers, and the white man grabbed me by the shoulder and knocked me out the door."

"A white man slapped me."

These illustrations indicate overt actions taken by majority group members in their rejection of Negro children; pain-punishment was being used as a method for reinforcing the idea of disapproval. The fact that these actions are directed by adults against children would tend to indicate that persons directing them are thwarted in attaining the status they wish in the larger society. Domination over someone else, a form of tyranny, supplies a short cut to satisfying the psychological need for power. It is improbable that these same individuals would attack an adult male Negro.

Aggressive behavior by white children in picking quarrels and fights, throwing stones, breaking toys, snatching belongings:

[3] Laurance F. Shaffer, *The Psychology of Adjustment.* Boston, Houghton Mifflin Company, 1936.

"I was going down the street and the white boy kicked me, and when I went to hit him he set his dog on me. I started running and the dog bit my ankle."

"Sure I fight white children 'cause they're always bothering me. When they start messin' with me we get in a fight. I want to kill 'em, kill 'em dead."

"Once we went on a hike and some white boys threw rocks at us and tried to spit on us."

"I had been to the Art Museum and was sitting on a bridge over some water in the park. Some white boys started throwing at me, then they came running up and tried to push me in."

"I go to the Center. The children get along all right in the Center, but when they get out on the street the white boys start picking on the colored boys. They like to fight."

"Sometimes we go to the park and over the mountains, and the white boys on the other side throw rocks at us. I was holding my airplane one day in the park and a white boy ran by real fast and knocked it out of my hand and broke it."

"Once a crowd of white boys caught a couple of colored boys and tied them to a tree and beat them."

"A bunch of white boys started throwing rocks at us. We started to run, then we turned around and got in a fight with them. We beat them up. That made up for everything, 'cause fighting is my hobby."

The instigation of conflicts by white children, without provocation other than the presence of particular individuals who represent an "out-group," would seem to indicate that attitudes have been absorbed by these children from a source whose authority they do not question. Dollard hypothesizes that aggression always follows frustrations.[4] Evidently, some children early absorb attitudes which cause them to perceive of the Negro as a threat to their well-being and, therefore, an object to be suppressed. Ego-strivings are satisfied through aggressive behavior.

Subtle manifestations

Discrimination with respect to rights and privileges; being denied access to situations because of being a Negro; lack of acceptance on basis of equality as another human being; unfair, injurious dis-

---

[4] John Dollard *et al., Frustration and Aggression.* New Haven, Yale University Press, 1931.

tinctions made because of identity as Negro; truthfulness doubted; expression of or signs interpreted to mean that Negro can't be trusted because he is a Negro:

"I went out to Coney Island and bought a ticket to go in the canoe. The man wouldn't let me get in. He said colored people couldn't ride on the water."

"I was riding my bicycle and got a flat. I took it in the station to get it fixed. The man wouldn't let me have no air, and he said he couldn't fix things for colored people."

"Our class went to a broadcast over WNYC, and afterwards the teachers took us to a place to eat. They wouldn't let us come in. We went to another one, and they wouldn't let us come in there either. I don't know what the man told the teacher, but she had to bring us back to a restaurant on 116th Street where we could eat. We never did feel right."

"One time I was visiting my grandmother, and she sent me after some coffee. The storeman got it for me, but when a white woman came in, he stopped waiting on me and he gave the white woman my coffee. I had to wait until he got through."

"The white boys and the colored boys got in a fight, and the cops came. They didn't say nothing to the white boys, but they started chasing us and told us to get on home."

"I was in the drugstore deciding which funny book to get. The man said, 'Don't pick that up.' The white children were looking through all of them, but I guess he thought I was going to steal it or get it dirty."

"I went in a roadside place to eat something because I was real hungry. The woman put my sandwich in a bag and told me to eat it outside. There were white people eating all over the place."

"The white children run all over the yard next door to us. One day my ball went over the fence. I went to get it and the lady called the police."

Discriminatory practice may be thought of as a form of defense devised to offset the upward mobility of a group which is seeking to end its suppression and to achieve integration. Inherent in such practice, which favors one group and rejects another, is an attitude of unfairness and an element of injustice.

Rude treatment. Discourteous, insulting behavior, ill-mannered treatment:

"One day I was swinging in the park and a white girl stuck out her tongue at me and wouldn't use the swing I had when I got through using it. She waited for a white girl to get through."

"One day I was in the park and a little white boy's ball bounced through the fence and rolled down the street. I went in and got it for him, but he didn't say nothing. Another time it did the same thing and he went after it. After he got back another boy said, 'Why didn't you let the nigger girl get it? You know you haven't got any business down there in their neighborhood.' "

"White children don't come out and tell you they don't want you around, but when you start playing games with them, they all stop."

"One time I went to the Automat with my folks. A white woman in there kept staring at us. Then she began making fun of us and laughing at us."

"White children laugh and make fun of my short hair."

"One day when we were going on a trip, a white woman got on the bus and said, 'Where are you going?' We told her this was the Youth Builders Club and we were going to a forum. She wanted to know if they asked questions at the forum. We told her yes. She said, 'Well, I have a question. Why don't you colored people go back to Africa where you belong?' "

"One day a boy was waving his handkerchief in school and the teacher told him to put it in the waste basket. Then she put her foot on it and stomped and stomped it."

"The white man in the store doesn't act nice. He throws your money at you, and sometimes it falls on the floor."

"I went up past Columbia University to the water. The people up by the river turned around and stared at us as if to say, 'What are you doing up here!' "

In these instances, individuals dramatize their thinking in more subtle behavior, which probably preserves their sense of decency in conduct, which in turn enables them to remain more at peace with their consciences than they might be if their rejecting behavior were more openly hostile, or if they abused the Negroes physically.

Indirect disparagement. Disparaging stereotypes in publications, movies, and radio:

". . . It makes me so mad just like I get when I walk into a five-and-dime store and see those real dark dolls with one black braid sticking out one way and one going another, and with a piece of red ribbon tied on one end of them."

"I don't like the movies with colored people in them. Colored people are as good as white people. Why put them down! They give them the simpler parts—something like under-hand jobs—that 'yes suh, boss' stuff. It's like being a servant all the time—someone who does all the stuff for you. To put it frankly, it makes you think of slavery."

"The movies always have such ole silly parts for colored people. There is a man who plays Charlie Chan's servant. He's always bucking his eyes and looking scary and acting crazy. One time he was on the elevator and the bottom of it started going down and he jumped up to the top of it and hung on. He looked real terrible. Then the bottom of the elevator came up and Charlie Chan was standing on it, and he said, 'Mr. Chan, what yo' all standin' on?' I guess he was supposed to be funny. The white people laughed, but my blood boiled."

"I don't like Negro characters on the radio. They make them sound so funny, so silly. They are always scary, afraid of things—ghosts, and things like that. I don't see why they take those parts. It's just making fun of themselves."

"I don't like the parts colored people have. They give them parts that make them seem inferior."

"I don't like some of the radio parts that colored people have. I don't like 'The Great Gildersleeve' program. I think Beulah is terrible. I don't like Amos and Andy. Colored people don't sound that way unless they are hoarse."

"I don't like the maid and servant parts colored people have. They're always 'busting suds.' It makes me ashamed. I don't like the radio parts either. In a play about Harry Jones and his family there is a colored woman who just loves white people so much she can't even stay at home and look after her own family. It makes me mad to hear that 'cause it ain't true."

"I don't like the parts they have. I don't like the way they look. I saw a man once, and he had a real black face and shiny head and white lips. The white people enjoyed it. I was ashamed. On the radio there is a program that comes on Wednesday evening. There is a white man that dresses up like a colored woman. I saw his picture once. He's real fat and black and talks funny like he thinks she talks. That really made me mad."

In indirect disparagement we find a subtle means of portraying traits, supposedly distinctive of Negroes, which are designed to be laughed at by others. The characteristics emphasized are those which support racial mores, and these are preserved through the media of movies, radio, and publications. The roles enacted tend to parallel the status of the Negro in the larger society of which he is a part.

The same procedure of categorizing, checking, tallying, and tabulating was used in connection with the statements of feelings, impulses toward the environment, and actual responses made. The results are presented in the following chapters.

RELIABILITY OF INTERVIEWS

Because of the nature of the material involved in a study of this kind, the reliability of data cannot be determined with certainty. However, to obtain an indication of the reliability of the responses, twelve children (two boys and two girls of each age group from ten through twelve) from the low income group in New York were interviewed a second time. The interval between interviews was ten weeks. It was observed that children tended to report recent experiences, so that in the event an experience had occurred the day before the second interview, that experience was likely to be related. There were few instances of this nature, however. In the second interview the investigator sometimes injected a key word of a previous report if the child omitted a previously reported experience.

It was also observed that a child might have reported having been called "nigger" on the first occasion, and "monkey chaser" or "black cracker" on the second. Even though specific names had been changed or added, the category label remained the same.

The replies of children in the second interview were classified in the categories already set up. A comparison was then made with their replies at the time of the first interview. In a total of 72 items compared, there were 66 instances of agreement. That is, 66 responses were classed in the same categories in the first and second interviews. Nine instances of change were noted, making the percentage of agreement 88 per cent.

A third interview was not attempted because there was evidence during the second interview that children were becoming some-what weary of the subject, and their attention wandered to discussions of a more pleasant nature.

Another matter that has a bearing on the value of the present results is the attitude shown by the children toward the interviewer. After an initial period necessary for gaining friendly rapport, children generally spoke freely and with vigor. The effect of the presence of other adults will be considered later. A few hesitated at first, as if the occurrence of such experiences was a reflection of a personal inadequacy. However, after a period such children usually spoke with less restraint. There was no attempt to cajole a child into talking. If he reported no unpleasant experiences, that report was accepted. Only one child, a member of the low income group in New York, showed any emotional stress. This child spoke with ease until he was asked the question, "Do you have a white teacher or a colored teacher?" At this point, he firmly closed his mouth and refused to say anything else.

Interviews lasted approximately 25 to 60 minutes. It is probable that the picture presented is more often characterized by omission than by invention. If interviews had extended over a longer period, more experiences might have been forthcoming.

Chapter Two

KINDS OF DIFFICULTIES REPORTED
BY CHILDREN

Problem 1

What are the problems which Negro children face because of their identity as Negroes?

Table III presents the findings of all children interviewed, and indicates the percentage of children who reported a given difficulty and the percentage of difficulties that fell in each category. Table IV presents the difficulties reported by boys and girls in lower and upper income groups in New York and St. Louis respectively. In these and other tables, categories described earlier are used. These include overt verbal manifestations such as ridicule, including name-calling and disparaging statements; overt actions such as physical ill-treatment on the part of white adults, and aggressive behavior on the part of white children; and the more subtle manifestations such as discriminatory practices, rude treatment, and indirect disparagement as found in movie and radio stereotypes.

The 90 children interviewed in New York reported a total of 272 negative experiences or difficulties, while 60 children in St. Louis reported 215. In all, 150 children reported a total of 487 difficulties.

Because there is a question as to whether the obtained frequencies in the categories are significantly different from the frequencies which one would get if the difficulties were distributed among the categories according to chance, the Chi-square test was employed. In instances in which the number in the cells did not meet Chi-square requirements, Yates's correction for continuity was applied. The Chi-square test was used to note significant differences in the number of difficulties reported rather than in the number of children reporting.

TABLE III

PERCENTAGE OF ALL CHILDREN REPORTING A GIVEN DIFFICULTY, AND PERCENTAGE OF
ALL REPORTED DIFFICULTIES IN EACH CATEGORY

Type of Difficulty	*Percentage of Children Reporting* (150)*	*Percentage of Total Difficulties Reported* (487)
Ridicule	70.6	28.9
Physical ill-treatment	10.0	4.3
Aggressive behavior	40.0	14.3
Rude treatment	17.3	6.5
Discrimination	31.3	17.0
Indirect disparagement	54.0	28.9

* Content of this and all subsequent tables is based on the population that is left after subtracting the 5 per cent who did not have problems. Although 150 children reported, only 143 reported difficulties.

TABLE IV

PERCENTAGE OF DIFFICULTIES EXPERIENCED IN EACH CATEGORY

Type of Difficulty	NEW YORK				ST. LOUIS			
	Lower Income		*Upper Income*		*Lower Income*		*Upper Income*	
	*B.**	*G.**	*B.*	*G.*	*B.*	*G.*	*B.*	*G.*
Number of difficulties reported	64	118	37	53	51	45	65	54
Ridicule	31	28	27	43	20	31	32	18
Physical ill-treatment	9	8	5	4	0	0	0	4
Aggressive behavior	12	8	32	9	24	9	14	11
Rude treatment	8	12	0	13	0	4	0	7
Discrimination	6	13	19	2	23	9	35	30
Indirect disparagement	33	31	16	28	33	47	18	30

* B = Boys, G = Girls, in all tables.

Problem 1a

Do difficulties faced by Negro children vary in number and kind with section?

It appears from Table IV that the difficulties faced by the children interviewed do not differ in kind with geographical section, but their frequency varied in relation to other factors. Girls in the lower income group in New York reported a larger number of difficulties than did the comparable group in St. Louis (Chi-square, 21.2). Upper income boys in St. Louis reported a larger number than did this group in New York (Chi-square, 20.1). Both differences are significant at the .01 level of probability (6.6).

Lower income boys and upper income girls showed no significant variation in the two cities in the number of difficulties reported.

In connection with these findings, it seems worth while to mention two observations. The girls of the lower income group in New York, when sought for interviews, were found either playing on the sidewalk while attending younger members of the family, or locked indoors looking after the house while their mothers worked. This early meeting of a cultural demand to accept mature responsibilities possibly results in a type of outgoing behavior. These girls were in general the most spontaneous of the New York children, talking freely and often at great length. The larger number of difficulties reported by them might be accounted for by the fact that they talked more freely about themselves and about the things which they had experienced.

On the other hand, the parents of upper income boys in New York showed little inclination in general to allow free participation by the children in the interviews. There appeared to be a tendency on their part to resist any situation which they felt might sensitize the children. This resulted in an air of restraint in some cases which might have served to depress the number of difficulties reported. This interference was avoided in St. Louis since few children were interviewed in the presence of their parents.

Such factors, which do not lend themselves to quantitative analysis, should, nevertheless, be kept in mind.

Incidentally, many New York parents in the upper income group spoke proudly of the white associates of their children in the private schools they attended, and of interracial visits and parties, and seemed to have aspiration levels for them which were best protected by segregating them from the masses of Negroes, thus tempering group identity.

Such parental behavior may indicate that, beyond a quantitative appraisal of difficulties met, factors associated with a given region are significant in providing unique social structures which allow for certain types of participation and which in turn give rise to particular thought patterns and attitudes peculiar to the region. For example, Negro membership in private white schools in New York, previously referred to, seems to lessen the interest of upper income Negroes of that city in identifying themselves as Negro, while the segregated schools of St. Louis may serve to sharpen this sense of identity. On the other hand, as will be indicated later, regional factors may be less significant than the values and beliefs of parents, whose attacks on social problems reflect the direction and power of their attitudes and reactions irrespective of the particular setting in which they live.

It also appears that factors associated with a given region may be significant in accenting social pressures. Although there is similarity in kind or pattern of difficulties in each setting, there is a difference in the intensity or repetition of appearance of particular patterns. Children in New York reported more often than did those in St. Louis the more subtle, indirect manifestations: rude, ill-mannered treatment such as staring and whispering (Chi-square, 8.9). Children in St. Louis reported more often behavior which, though having elements of the inferential, was more overt in character and more directly aimed (Chi-square, 20.1). (.01 level of probability in both cases, 6.6.)

One of the most persistent types of difficulty reported in St. Louis was that related to eating privileges. Though it is understood that Negroes are generally restricted from larger white restaurants, the policies of small lunch stands seem confusing. Boys seeking to be served at these met with the following forms of response: definite refusal, restriction to outdoor eating if sold food, and service indoors provided they remain standing. The following statement of an upper income boy is typical: "I was tired and thirsty when we came back from the hike and I saw a little old store at the side of the road. I went in and asked for a drink of water, and the man said, 'I haven't got any broken dishes and I don't keep any dirty pans!'"

Rejections on street cars were also prominently reported. According to these reports, white passengers tell Negro children not to sit beside them, push them aside to make room for other white persons, and remain standing if the child has been seated first, refusing the vacant seat beside him.

Evidently at this age cultural patterns have not been completely learned, and children expose themselves to difficulties in the process of learning. These social learnings are reinforced not so much through the behavior of parents as through the punishing effects of the wider environment.

The amount of ridicule and aggression faced does not differ significantly with region: the discrepancy between the two distributions is no greater than would be expected by chance which occurs in random sampling. This similarity is evidently due to the cultural dissemination of a common attitude which results in the emergence of these like patterns with similar strength, irrespective of region.

Negative reactions mobilized by movie and radio stereotypes are experienced with the same intensity in the two regions. As will be shown later, there appears to be a greater difference in the reactions of individuals within the two cities.

While Table IV indicates the frequency with which specific difficulties appear and are reported by all the children in a given sample, Table V indicates the percentage of children in each city reporting a particular type of difficulty.

TABLE V

PERCENTAGE OF CHILDREN REPORTING DIFFICULTIES IN EACH OF THE CATEGORIES

	NEW YORK				ST. LOUIS			
Type of Difficulty	*Lower Income*		*Upper Income*		*Lower Income*		*Upper Income*	
	B.	*G.*	*B.*	*G.*	*B.*	*G.*	*B.*	*G.*
Number of children reporting	30	30	15	15	15	15	15	15
Ridicule	43	63	67	100	67	93	100	67
Physical ill-treatment	7	23	13	13	0	0	0	13
Aggression	27	17	47	60	80	27	60	40
Rude treatment	13	30	0	47	0	13	0	27
Discrimination	13	17	27	7	73	13	93	40
Indirect disparagement	43	73	20	47	67	87	40	47

In New York, 63 per cent of the children, the largest group reporting the same kind of experience, reported direct ridicule, and 15 per cent, the smallest group, reported discriminatory practices. In St. Louis, 81 per cent of the children, the largest group, reported ridicule, and 2 per cent, the smallest group, reported rude treatment. In the tabulation of both the frequency of difficulties reported and the frequency of children reporting difficulties, ridicule stands a dominating pattern.

Problem 1b

Do difficulties faced by Negro children differ in number and kind with socio-economic level within each city?

If we examine Table V, which records the percentages of children reporting difficulties and the nature of the difficulties, it appears that in the lower income group in New York ridicule, both direct and indirect, is reported by the largest number of boys. The smallest number, or 7 per cent, reported physical ill-treatment. The largest number of low income girls in New York, or 73 per cent, reported negative reactions to movie and radio stereotypes. One of the smallest groups reported discriminating practices. Of the upper income boys in New York, 67 per cent, the largest number in that group, reported ridicule. All of the upper income girls reported ridicule. The smallest number, 7 per cent, reported discriminatory practices.

Upper income children in New York reported more often than lower income children that they were ridiculed and attacked by white children. Lower income children were more disturbed by movie and radio stereotypes.

These findings tend to show the relationship between the kind and extent of contacts which groups have and the types of difficulties that emerge. In the absence of firsthand experience, because of the comparative isolation of the setting of low income children, stereotypes of the Negro presented in publications, movies, and radio become the main avenues used by them in evaluating the attitudes of white persons toward them. Reports of upper income children would seem to indicate that mere proximity does not make for understanding.

In St. Louis, as shown in Table V, the two largest groups of low income boys, 80 per cent and 73 per cent respectively, reported aggressive behavior on the part of white children and discriminatory practices. None reported rude treatment. The largest number of low income girls, 93 per cent, reported ridicule, and 87 per cent reported disturbing reactions to movie and radio stereotypes. Discrimination was reported by the smallest number. All of the upper income boys in St. Louis reported ridicule, and 93 per cent reported discriminatory practices. No boy reported rude treatment. The largest number of upper income girls, 67 per cent, reported ridicule, and 40 per cent reported discriminatory practices.

In St. Louis, direct ridicule is the difficulty reported by the largest number of children in both income groups. In the upper income group, the next largest number reported discriminatory practices. In the lower income group, the next largest number reported indirect disparagement.

As previously indicated, discriminatory practices, a more overt pattern, are more obvious in St. Louis than in New York, and rude treatment, a more subtle pattern, is more prevalent in New York than in St. Louis.

In considering the number of difficulties reported in New York City, rather than the number of children reporting, socio-economic level does not appear significant. In other words, there was no significant difference in the number of difficulties reported by lower and upper income children (Chi-square, 11.8; .01 level of probability, 13.3). A revealing difference, however, was found in relation to the nature of the patterns reported. While 53 per cent of the difficulties reported by lower income children were of a less overt, more inferential, nature such as rude treatment and indirect disparagement, only 35 per cent of the reports of upper income children were of this nature. This may indicate that lower income children in this city show a greater sensitivity than those of the upper income group, and that the latter are less likely to notice behavior unless there is active face-to-face exchange of words or blows. On the other hand, it may indicate that limitation of contact with white persons tends to limit ability to judge discriminatingly with reference to motives for conduct. Extensive contacts, such as upper income children have, may make them less conscious of the behavior in white persons which lower income children tend to judge as purposely unkind.

As a matter of fact, an analysis of reports of lower income children in New York showed some reactions which might have been inappropriate under the circumstances of the situation. For example, one child said, "When we went to the museum, we went downstairs to eat, and the colored children had a bad looking table with old rough-looking boards, and the white children had a high-class-looking table. When I went over to say something to a boy at the table where the white children were, the lady said, 'Go on back where you belong.' It sure did make me feel bad." Another child reported as follows with reference to a museum trip: "The white children had their coats all hanging up nice on hooks, and the colored children had to pile theirs on top of each other any old kind of way. It made me mad." In both instances, first arrivals might have taken advantage of the best offerings of the setting. The attendant mentioned in the first illustration might have been intent on keeping groups together in order to avoid confusion. Such reactions, however, even under these conditions, would indicate the presence of some factor or factors, operating in the environment in which these children live, which mobilize threats to their personal security and toward which a defense is developed. Even in the absence of firsthand experiences, children may take on ways of thinking by identifying with members of their family and group who have experienced ill-treatment. The variety of meanings which the individual abstracts from cultural inferences depends upon the social forces in his life pattern which accompany his introduction to them. Evidently, experiences of some kind have been responsible for the development of such feelings of sensitivity.

More reactions to movie and radio stereotypes were reported by lower income children than by upper income children. The relationship was significant at the .02 level of probability.

As shown in Table VI, 43 per cent of the lower income children in New York, the largest number in that group, reported from one to two experiences, and 8 per cent reported seven or more. Forty-three per cent of the upper income group, the largest number in that group, reported between three and four difficulties.

In New York, then, the majority of lower income children reported between one and two difficulties, while the majority of upper income children reported between three and four. This may be due in part to factors of proximity and availability. Upper income children, as suggested earlier, do not live for the most part in the lower Harlem area which is a narrowly confined, definitely

Negro community. The exposure is therefore greater through the larger number of daily contacts. Further, it was found that in New York only 38 per cent of the lower income children had ever been in a white neighborhood.

In St. Louis, there appears to be no significant difference between the number and kind of difficulties reported in the two income groups, although the upper income children reported a slightly larger number than the lower income group. Upper income children seem to encounter discriminatory practices more often than do lower income children. The latter express negative reactions to movie and radio stereotypes more often. This reaction to stereotypes is again significant at the .02 level of probability.

TABLE VI

NUMBER OF DIFFICULTIES REPORTED PER CHILD IN LOWER AND UPPER INCOME GROUPS

| Number of Difficulties | NEW YORK | | | | | | ST. LOUIS | | | | | |
| | Lower Income | | | Upper Income | | | Lower Income | | | Upper Income | | |
	B.	G.	%	B.	G.	%	B.	G.	%	B.	G.	%
0	4	1	8	1	1	7	0	0	0	0	0	0
1–2	16	10	43	9	2	37	4	5	30	2	4	20
3–4	8	7	25	4	9	43	8	7	50	8	10	60
5–6	2	7	15	1	2	10	2	2	13	5	1	20
7 or more ...	0	5	8	0	1	3	1	1	7	0	0	0

Table VI also indicates that no child in the low income group in St. Louis reported no difficulties, while 50 per cent, the largest number in the group, reported between three and four. In the upper income group in St. Louis, again no child reported no difficulties of the nature investigated, while 60 per cent, the largest number, reported from three to four. The majority of children at both income levels experienced between three and four difficulties.

In St. Louis there are no residential boundaries as definitely demarcated as are those of the lower Harlem area in New York. This latter area, set off by the highly accented, cliffed border at Morningside Avenue on the west and the park at 110th Street on the south, presents physical as well as psychological barriers to greater movement outside the area. In St. Louis there is greater ease of movement, and children in general move about the larger city environs more often. This may account for the fact that no child in St. Louis reported having escaped all forms of social pressure.

The average number of difficulties reported per child was three for both cities. It should be stated, in passing, that the number of difficulties cannot be taken as a criterion for judging the degree of personal disturbance resulting from group pressures. Mere enumeration cannot indicate the intensity of the experience. For example, the child who was burned on purpose by a white cigar smoker and told that he thought her hand was an ash tray, and who said she was ashamed she looked that way, would need only one such experience to develop intense attitudes regarding white persons, and regarding herself in relation to them.

The fact that some children report one experience while others report five or six may be due to personality differences or varying reactions which are more allied to individual make-up than to external conditions. The greater amount of movement and extension of contacts by some children may also account in part for the difference.

Incidentally, the experiences reported by children attending private schools in New York were in "better taste" than those reported by others. No child reported having been called "nigger," or any of the other epithets commonly reported, while at school. A remark such as "You are not an American citizen because you are a Negro," and the telling of "old colored man" stories and jokes were typical of the kinds of pressures met in these settings. However, they were reported as equally objectionable.

Problem 1c

Do the number and kind of experiences reported vary according to sex?

In the lower income group in New York there is no significant difference between the frequencies of reports of boys and girls in such traits as aggression, physical ill-treatment, ridicule, rude treatment, and discrimination. Girls in this group, however, reported more negative reactions to movie and radio stereotypes than did boys.

In the upper income group in New York boys and girls reported similarly on the frequency of appearance of patterns of ridicule, physical ill-treatment, aggression, discrimination, and indirect disparagement. Rude treatment was reported by girls but not by boys.

Table VI indicates, however, that a larger number of boys than girls in New York reported four or fewer difficulties, while a larger number of girls reported more than four. In other words, while 10 per cent of the boys reported more than four difficulties, 47 per cent of the girls reported more than this number.

In the St. Louis group there is no significant difference in reports of boys and girls in relation to the kind and frequency of difficulties met. There also seems to be a greater similarity than difference in the distribution of difficulties per child relative to sex. As indicated in Table VI, 17 per cent of the boys and 10 per cent of the girls reported more than four experiences each.

Generally, there appears to be no sex bias in attitudes held and behavior directed by majority group members toward these children, since the frequencies with which girls and boys have these experiences are about the same. One gathers from these data that there exists a common pattern or a whole which includes all children regardless of sex, but that out of this generality, girls tend to abstract more specifics of a subtle, or inferential, nature than do boys. This is evidenced in the fact that girls react more often to indirect disparagement and behavior judged ill-mannered and rude. This, together with the fact that some girls report a larger number of difficulties per person, may indicate some differences in sensitivity.

SUMMARY

Of the 150 children interviewed, 95 per cent had experienced situations which they interpreted as problems in Negro–white relations. Of this number, 77 per cent received threats to personal security through channels of ridicule, 56 per cent through movie and radio stereotypes, 41 per cent through aggressive behavior on the part of white children, 33 per cent through discriminatory situations, 18 per cent through rude, ill-mannered behavior, and 11 per cent through physical ill-treatment by white adults.

Of the 487 difficulties reported by these children, 28 per cent were of the nature of ridicule, 28 per cent negative reactions to movie and radio stereotypes, 17 per cent discrimination, 14 per cent aggressive behavior by white children, 7 per cent rude treatment, and 4 per cent physical ill-treatment by white adults.

Five per cent of the children reported no difficulties. This group consisted of five boys and two girls, all of New York. Four boys and one girl were at the low income level, and one boy and one girl at the upper income level. One cannot account for the presence of this group with absolute assurance; however, some conjectures can be made. It is possible that in some instances there was a genuine statement of fact. Parental protectiveness and location within the community may have served as shields against encounters. On the other hand, lack of optimum conditions, in both the individual approached and the interview setting, may have been operative. These conditions would include lack of understanding of questions, limited facility in the use of language, inadequate rapport between child and interviewer, and insufficient motivation for response. It might be stated that the interviewer was conscious of some of these factors in some instances, particularly with low income children. Incidentally, some general restraint in talking about the suggested topics might have been present because of previous conditioning.

It appears that the most persistent pressure is ridicule, for it reaches more children and appears as a prevalent pattern in the total list of difficulties. Sensitivity to this pressure creates a demand for adequate adjustive techniques to offset its effect.

Evidently the folk culture with reference to the Negro in New York and St. Louis is highly similar: the traits or action patterns of majority group members in both cities appear to be a reflection of the same basic attitudes. The prevalent rejecting technique used by the dominant group in New York, however, appears to be more disguised, less overt, than that in St. Louis. Difficulties reported show variation in magnitude as the locality changes.

Generally, the study of the distribution of difficulties in relation to socio-economic level shows that group differences are negligible. The cultural environment, in regions of the kind studied, is dominated by attitudes which label all Negro children without regard to background, and directs behavior to all alike.

Sex does not appear to be a factor related to the presence or absence of difficulties. However, manifestations from which an unfavorable attitude may be inferred are noticed more by girls than by boys.

Low income children who live in closely knit ethnic communities appear to pay relatively more attention to implied prejudice (such as rude treatment and indirect disparagement) than do upper income children, perhaps because they are, not more sensitive necessarily, but more shielded from direct contact. Findings also suggest that the experiences that befall Negro children are influenced, in part, by the type of adjoining white neighborhood.

Lack of direct contact and concrete social experiences causes the individual to rely upon other available cultural symbols for the patterning of attitudes. Such sources may be unreliable indices for use in evaluating and judging. For example, lower income children, who have few personal contacts, expressed a dislike for white people because of the roles which are assigned to Negroes in movies and radio.

Segregated communities tend to breed cultural isolates and a consciousness of differences and stigmas attached to them. Seventy-two per cent of the children in the low income group in Harlem had never been in a white neighborhood, and none expressed a desire to go. Statements such as "I'd rather be with my own kind," "I'm scared of white people," and "They stare at you as if to say, 'You haven't got any business here'" were typical.

Proximity may provide opportunities for social communication, but it is not necessarily conducive to understanding. Other factors may operate to offset the understanding which could develop.

Chapter Three

FEELINGS AROUSED IN CHILDREN BY DIFFICULTIES THEY ENCOUNTERED

Problem 2

What inner feelings are associated with these experiences?

It has been shown that similar difficulties prevail among social groups irrespective of geographical section. In order to determine individual reactions to environmental conditions, children were questioned with reference to feelings attending these experiences. Table VII presents the percentages of children reporting feeling responses, and the percentage of feeling responses that fall in a given category. Table VIII presents the kinds of feelings and the frequencies of their appearance in the two cities. Feelings reported may be described as resentment, inferiority, fear, and indifference. Some children were unable to express their feelings in words, and said, "I don't know how I felt." A statement such as "It didn't make no difference" might be a cloak for basic inferiority feelings; on the other hand, it might be a true expression of feeling.

Of the total number of children reporting, 69 per cent reported resentment, 47 per cent inferiority feelings, 6 per cent fear reactions, and 3 per cent indifference. Of the total number of feeling responses reported, 57 per cent were categorized as resentment, 38 per cent as inferiority, 3 per cent as fear reactions, and 1 per cent as indifference. In the picture as a whole, resentment appears to be the dominant feeling tone experienced, having been reported by the largest number of children, and appearing as a dominant pattern in the total list of feeling responses.

Problem 2a

Are kinds of feelings related to section?

It appears that similar problems provoke similar feelings regardless of region. (Chi-square, 1.2; .01 level of probability, 6.3)

TABLE VII

PERCENTAGE OF ALL CHILDREN REPORTING A GIVEN FEELING RESPONSE,
AND PERCENTAGE OF ALL FEELING RESPONSES THAT FELL IN A
GIVEN CATEGORY

Type of Feeling Response	*Percentage of Children Reporting* (150)	*Percentage of Total Feeling Responses Reported* (487)
Resentment	69	57
Inferiority: shame, hurt feelings, embarrassment, funny feelings	47	38
Fear	6	3
Indifference	3	1
Unable to articulate feeling experienced	3	1

Problem 2b

Are feeling tones or emotions related to income level?

In the lower income group in New York, the largest number of boys, 80 per cent, expressed resentment, and the smallest, 3 per cent, fear. The largest number of girls in this group, 70 per cent, expressed inferiority feeling, and the two smallest groups, 10 per cent each, expressed fear and indifference.

Resentment seemed to be the dominant feeling tone of lower income boys in New York in instances of ridicule, physical ill-treatment, aggression, and indirect disparagement. Inferiority feelings most often accompany instances of rude treatment and discrimination. Lower income girls showed resentment more than any other emotion in relation to ridicule, physical ill-treatment, aggressive behavior, and indirect disparagement.

In the upper income group in New York, the largest number of boys, 87 per cent, reported resentment, and the smallest, 7 per cent, fear. The largest number of upper income girls, 67 per cent, expressed resentment, and the smallest, 7 per cent, indifference.

Boys in the upper income group in New York indicated resentment as the prevalent feeling tone in relation to all situations. Upper income girls indicated resentment as a prevalent emotional reaction in instances of ridicule and aggression. Inferiority feelings were prominent in cases of indirect disparagement, rude treatment, and discrimination.

TABLE VIII

PERCENTAGE OF CHILDREN REPORTING EACH OF THE VARIOUS FEELINGS

Type of Feeling Response	NEW YORK				ST. LOUIS			
	Lower Income		*Upper Income*		*Lower Income*		*Upper Income*	
	B.	*G.*	*B.*	*G.*	*B.*	*G.*	*B.*	*G.*
Number of children reporting	30	30	15	15	15	15	15	15
Resentment	80	63	87	67	67	47	80	53
Inferiority feelings	27	70	20	60	47	80	40	33
Fear	3	10	7	0	0	13	7	7
Indifference	0	10	0	7	7	0	0	0
Unable to articulate feeling experienced	7	0	0	0	0	13	7	0

TABLE IX

PERCENTAGES OF VARIOUS FEELINGS EXPERIENCED WHEN DIFFICULTIES WERE ENCOUNTERED

Type of Feeling Response	NEW YORK				ST. LOUIS			
	Lower Income		*Upper Income*		*Lower Income*		*Upper Income*	
	B.	*G.*	*B.*	*G.*	*B.*	*G.*	*B.*	*G.*
Number of reactions reported	64	118	37	53	51	45	65	54
Resentment	69	46	83	55	65	20	68	65
Inferiority feelings	26	47	14	43	33	67	28	33
Fear	2	4	3	0	0	9	2	2
Indifference	0	2	0	2	2	0	0	0
Unable to articulate feeling experienced	3	0	0	0	0	4	2	0

When we consider the number of instances reported rather than the number of children reporting, Table IX shows that feelings of inferiority, fear, resentment, and indifference were present at both upper and lower income levels. The frequency of appearance of these reactions showed no variation beyond that of chance.

In St. Louis, as indicated in Table VIII, the largest group of low income boys, 67 per cent, expressed anger reactions. None mentioned fear. The largest number of low income girls, 80 per cent, spoke of inferiority feelings, while the smallest number mentioned fear.

In the upper income group the largest number of boys and girls, 80 per cent and 53 per cent respectively, mentioned resentment, and the smallest groups, 2 per cent of both boys and girls, mentioned fear.

Table IX indicates that some variation in reported feelings appears in the comparison of socio-economic groups. There were a significantly larger number of inferiority feelings in the lower income group than in the upper (Chi-square, 7.9). In the upper income group, there were more instances of resentment reported (Chi-square, 10.1). (.01 level of probability in both instances, 6.6.)

It is profitable to consider the relation of feelings aroused to the type of difficulty faced. Lower income boys in St. Louis expressed resentment as a dominant emotion in response to aggressive behavior and indirect disparagement. Inferiority feelings most often accompanied discriminatory practices, and were prevalent in ridicule. With lower income girls, inferiority was the dominant feeling, and was caused most often by ridicule, rude treatment, discrimination, and indirect disparagement.

Upper income boys experienced resentment in all difficulties except discrimination, in which instance inferiority feelings were prevalent. Upper income girls felt resentment more than any other emotion in relation to all difficulties except rude treatment. In this case inferiority feelings were prevalent.

Problem 2c

Are frequencies of various feelings aroused related to sex?

In the lower income group in New York, the incidence of feelings of resentment and fear was unrelated to sex. Girls, however, expressed more inferiority reactions than boys (Chi-square, 7.0). In the upper income group in New York, boys expressed more resentment than girls (Chi-square, 8.3), while girls expressed more feelings of inferiority (Chi-square, 9.1). (.01 level of probability in each instance, 6.6.)

In St. Louis, low income boys expressed more resentment than did girls, and girls reported more instances of inferiority feelings.

The Chi-square value in the first instance is 23.4, in the second, 11.0; the .01 level of probability is 6.6.

In the upper income group in St. Louis, sex does not appear to be related to the frequency of particular feelings experienced. Boys and girls did not differ significantly in the number of instances in which feelings of inferiority, resentment, and fear were provoked.

Generally, girls expressed more inferiority feelings than boys.

SUMMARY

It appears that resentment is aroused most often in situations involving ridicule, physical ill-treatment, aggression, and indirect disparagement. Two groups which showed exceptions were low income girls in St. Louis, who reacted to ridicule with inferiority feelings, and upper income girls in New York, who reacted to indirect disparagement with inferiority feelings.

As far as all children are concerned, inferiority feelings most often accompany situations involving discrimination and rude treatment.

Fear, mentioned least, occurred most often in response to aggression, and was expressed more by girls than by boys. The genuineness of the low mention of fear may be questioned. It is possible that fear was a component of both inferiority feelings and resentment, not introspectively differentiated by the subjects.

As previously stated, low income children reported more negative reactions to movie and radio stereotypes than did upper income children. In St. Louis, they also reported more inferiority feelings. Low income children may consciously or unconsciously identify with the characters who play servant roles and may interpret these roles as an implication of inferior status.

It was also observed that girls who reported a greater number of less tangible difficulties, such as rude treatment and indirect disparagement, also reported more feelings of inferiority than boys. This may indicate that in the process of development girls tend toward a heightened awareness of self, such self-reference operating prominently in interpreting social phenomena. Or, it may suggest that the threshold of response for boys and girls differs in relation to particular stimuli. In a sense there seems to be a parallel between low income children in general and girls in their susceptibility to social stimuli and emotional conditioning. No broad claim is made here for a generalization concerning the greater sensitivity of girls, but only a statement of possibility as revealed by the data.

The dominant emotional reaction to difficulties as reported by boys was resentment. One may reasonably expect that attitudes held by these boys toward majority group members have negative emotional weighting, and that such attitudes will tend to persist unless the nature of subsequent life contacts is such as to offset the emotional weighting.

Chapter Four

KINDS OF IMPULSES AROUSED

Problem 3

When the children are faced with such experiences, what impulses are aroused? What do they feel like doing?

As shown above, feelings of resentment and inferiority were the ones reported most frequently by the children of both groups in the two cities. These feelings tend to be accompanied by impulses of some sort, directed toward the disturbing environmental elements. Children expressed a desire to fight, to argue, or to accept or ignore. To accept or ignore means that children stated they felt like "doing nothing." In about 5 per cent of the instances reported, children were unable to articulate their impulses, stating, "I don't know what I felt like doing."

Of the children reporting, Table X shows that 47 per cent reported a desire to fight, 36 per cent a desire to argue, 50 per cent a willingness to accept or ignore, and 17 per cent uncertainty as to what they felt like doing. Of the impulses reported in relation to situations encountered, 29 per cent were expressed as a desire to fight, 28 per cent as a desire to argue, and 37 per cent as a desire

TABLE X

Percentage of All Children Reporting Impulses in a Given Category, and Percentage of All Reported Impulses that Fell in Each Category

Type of Impulse	*Percentage of Children Reporting* (150)	*Percentage of Impulses in Each Category* (487)
To fight	47	29
To argue	36	28
To accept	50	37
Unable to articulate impulse	17	5

to accept or ignore; in 5 per cent of the instances there was an inability to state what the impulse had been.

TABLE XI

PERCENTAGES OF VARIOUS IMPULSES EXPERIENCED WHEN DIFFICULTIES
WERE ENCOUNTERED

| Type of Impulse | NEW YORK | | | | ST. LOUIS | | | |
| | Lower Income | | Upper Income | | Lower Income | | Upper Income | |
	B.	G.	B.	G.	B.	G.	B.	G.
Number of impulses reported	64	118	37	53	51	45	65	54
To fight	36	12	59	34	53	20	25	26
To argue	12	30	8	38	20	13	42	46
To accept	41	50	27	26	27	67	28	20
Unable to articulate impulse	11	8	5	2	0	0	5	7

Problem 3a

Are impulses toward the environment related to section?

Reports of low income children, as shown in Table XI, indicate that impulses to fight, to argue, and to accept appear with about the same frequency in New York and St. Louis, with no significant variation. Upper income boys in New York, however, wanted to fight more often than did upper income boys in St. Louis (Chi-square value, 12.2). Upper income boys in St. Louis expressed a desire to argue more often than did those in New York (Chi-square, 13.0; .01 level of probability, 6.6).

The frequency of the expressed desire to do nothing was unrelated to region. New York and St. Louis girls in both upper and lower income groups reported similar frequencies for impulses aroused. They did not differ significantly in desires to fight, to argue, or to accept.

Problem 3b

Is there a relationship between the kinds of impulses aroused and socio-economic level?

In the lower income group in New York, as shown in Table XII, the largest number of boys, 60 per cent, wanted to fight and the smallest, 20 per cent, wanted to argue. The largest number of girls, 60 per cent, wanted to accept, and the smallest, 30 per cent, wanted to fight back.

TABLE XII

PERCENTAGES OF CHILDREN REPORTING IMPULSES IN THE VARIOUS CATEGORIES

	NEW YORK				ST. LOUIS			
Type of Impulse	*Lower Income*		*Upper Income*		*Lower Income*		*Upper Income*	
	B.	G.	B.	G.	B.	G.	B.	G.
Number of children report-ing	30	30	15	15	15	15	15	15
To fight	60	30	73	40	67	33	47	33
To argue	20	53	20	60	27	13	53	40
To accept	67	60	33	40	40	73	33	27
Unable to articulate impulse	27	30	13	7	0	0	20	27

In the upper income group in New York, the largest number of boys, 73 per cent, had an impulse to fight when difficulties were encountered, and the smallest, 20 per cent, wanted to argue. The largest group of upper income girls, 60 per cent, wanted to argue back, and the smallest groups, 40 per cent in each, wanted to fight or accept.

In relation to the frequency of appearance of impulses rather than the number of children expressing them, socio-economic level is not significant in the case of the New York boys. Girls, however, did show a difference. Low income girls in New York expressed a desire to do nothing more often than did upper income girls. A highly significant Chi-square value of 21.6 was indicated; .01 level of probability, 6.6.

Some relationships between particular difficulties and impulses directed toward the environment may be pointed out. It appears that lower income boys in New York wanted to fight most often in instances of ridicule, physical ill-treatment, and aggression, and to do nothing most often in instances of indirect disparagement and rude treatment. Lower income girls had an impulse to fight most often in response to aggression. They felt like doing nothing most often in cases of rude treatment, discrimination, and indirect disparagement.

Upper income boys in New York had a desire to fight most often in instances of ridicule, physical ill-treatment, aggression, and discrimination, and to do nothing most often in cases of indirect disparagement. Upper income girls wanted to fight in cases of aggression, to argue in instances of ridicule, discrimination, and rude treatment, and to do nothing in instances of physical ill-treatment and indirect disparagement.

In St. Louis, also, some variations relative to income level are noted. Upper income boys wanted to argue more often than did lower income boys (Chi-square, 7.7; .01 level of probability, 6.6). Upper income girls wanted to argue more than did lower income girls (Chi-square, 12.3), while the latter felt like doing nothing more often. The Chi-square value in the latter case is 21.6, both instances being significant at the .01 level of probability, 6.6.

Here again, the nature of the impulse aroused varies in relation to specific situations. It appears that low income boys felt like fighting most often in situations involving ridicule and aggression, and doing nothing most often in instances of indirect disparagement. The latter, however, was also a prevalent reaction in case of aggression and discrimination.

In the upper income group in St. Louis, boys had a desire to argue more often than any other impulse, and wished to do so most often in cases of ridicule and discrimination. They felt like fighting in instances of aggression and indirect disparagement. With upper income girls, the desire to argue was also quite noticeable, and was felt most often in response to ridicule and discrimination. It was also prevalent in cases of rude treatment. The desire to do nothing was felt most often as a reaction to indirect disparagement.

Problem 3c

Is there a relationship between sex and impulses toward the environment?

Lower income boys in New York reported more instances of wanting to fight than did lower income girls (Chi-square, 14.8). Girls in this group wanted to argue more often than did boys (Chi-square, 7.3; .01 level of probability, 6.6). The desire to do nothing was found as frequently among boys as among girls; sex would seem to be unrelated to this impulse.

In the upper income group, boys wanted to fight more often than did girls, the difference being significant at the .02 level of probability. Girls wanted to argue more often than did boys (corrected Chi-square, 8.6). Again, there was no significant difference in the frequencies of boys' and girls' desires to accept or do nothing.

In the low income group of St. Louis, boys had a desire to fight more often than did girls (Chi-square, 15.2). Girls tended toward doing nothing more often (Chi-square, 14.8; .01 level of probability, 6.6 in both instances). There was no significant difference in the incidence of desire to argue.

Upper income boys and girls in St. Louis showed no significant variation on any of the traits.

SUMMARY

In the absence of quantitative analysis, the intensity of the stimuli of ridicule, aggression, and physical ill-treatment is indicated by the fact that feelings of resentment, and impulses to fight, are most often aroused. Indirect disparagement also aroused resentment, but the impulse it most often aroused was that of acceptance. In the case of intangibles of this nature there may be a lack of mental mechanism for structuring defense, or no insight into possible methods of control. The remoteness of the source probably accounts for the lack of imagery. These are generalities postulated on the basis of the reports of children in both regions.

Boys, with one exception, showed no significant difference in the frequency with which they felt impelled to fight, argue, and accept. Upper income boys in St. Louis wanted to argue more often than did lower income boys.

Lower income girls, in addition to reporting more difficulties of an inferential nature and indicating more inferiority feelings, also wanted to accept more often. Some significance must be attached to the factor of being a girl and being reared in a less privileged environment, for these findings suggest greater susceptibility to inferences, less feeling of security of self, and less evidence of desire to reduce strains in social relations through positive action.

From these data, it appears that lower income children show no more aggressiveness in their impulses toward the environment than do upper income children. A greater tendency toward inertia seems, in fact, better to describe their reactions in Negro–white relations.

These findings, however, do not agree in this respect with those of other studies. Davis and Dollard noted on the part of lower class children rather consistent patterns of aggressiveness which distinguished them from upper class children.[1] As mentioned in the introductory remarks, the sample represented in this study may not include the more forward or aggressive members of the lower income group because children of this type probably do not attend the community centers from which names were secured. Another factor may be age level differences. Davis and Dollard deal mainly with adolescent youth, while this study is confined to a lower age level. There is the possibility that patterns of thinking toward majority group members are still in the process of being formulated at the ages of ten through twelve years, and have not yet crystallized into definite impulses of an aggressive nature.

[1] Allison Davis and John Dollard, *Children of Bondage*. Washington, D. C., American Council on Education, 1940.

Chapter Five

OVERT RESPONSES TO DIFFICULTIES

Problem 4

What overt responses do these children make to the diffi-culties reported?

The factors or stimuli here described as difficulties are likely to have consequences in some form of overt social conduct. It is likely that security systems will be established and that defenses will be mobilized, all of which find expression in social form. In speaking evaluatively of such responses, it is necessary to keep in mind that susceptibility to environmental stimuli depends upon the state of the organism at a particular time. Conversely, the state of the organism is influenced by the environment.

It is realized that these two factors have a great influence on the nature of the response made. In general, however, the Negro child in his daily living is, where white persons are involved, operating in a field in which relatively stable attitudes toward him exist. These attitudes in most instances reflect feelings of domination, and may engender feelings of restraint rather than those of security. It is therefore possible that whenever a Negro child, of an age and region comparable to those represented here, finds himself in a public setting in which such symbols of domination are present, he is likely, whatever the particular state of the organism, to be mentally and emotionally geared for defense. The following reports of kinds of responses made may be fairly indicative of behavior expectations (Tables XIII, XIV, XV).

In considering the total number of responses made to specific difficulties, we find that fighting occurred in 10 per cent of the cases, arguing in 7 per cent, and withdrawal in 82 per cent. In the accounting of children, it appears that 24 per cent of the children

TABLE XIII

PERCENTAGE OF ALL CHILDREN REPORTING A GIVEN OVERT RESPONSE, AND
PERCENTAGE OF ALL REPORTED RESPONSES THAT FELL IN EACH CATEGORY

Type of Response	*Number of Children Reporting* (150)	*Number of Total Responses Reported* (487)
Fought	24	10
Argued	18	7
Withdrew	75	82

actually fought, 18 per cent of them argued, and 75 per cent of them withdrew.

Problem 4a

Are kinds of response patterns related to section?

Lower income children in the two cities showed no significant variation in the frequency of fighting, arguing, and withdrawing.

Upper income boys in New York fought more often than did those in St. Louis (Chi-square, 14.2). Those in St. Louis withdrew more often (Chi-square, 12.4). This may suggest a difference in relations between white and Negro in New York: there may be a greater feeling of equality on the part of upper income boys in this section. Although not frequently, upper income girls in New York did fight back sometimes, in contrast to the corresponding group in St. Louis. The St. Louis girls did more withdrawing. (Chi-square value is 7.7; the .01 level of probability in all instances is 6.6.)

Problem 4b

Are responses related to socio-economic level?

In New York City, socio-economic level seems unrelated to actual responses made by boys in the two groups. There was no significant variation in the amounts of arguing, fighting, and withdrawing done. Although upper income boys reported slightly more fighting, the difference was not significant at the .05 level of probability. The findings are indicated in Table XIV.

TABLE XIV

PERCENTAGES OF VARIOUS OVERT RESPONSES MADE WHEN DIFFICULTIES
WERE ENCOUNTERED

Type of Response	NEW YORK				ST. LOUIS			
	Lower Income		*Upper Income*		*Lower Income*		*Upper Income*	
	B.	G.	B.	G.	B.	G.	B.	G.
Number of responses reported	64	118	37	53	51	45	65	54
Fought	20	4	28	9	18	4	6	0
Argued	5	5	3	21	6	13	5	7
Withdrew	75	91	69	70	76	82	89	92

Upper income girls argued and fought more often than lower income girls, while the latter withdrew more often (Chi-square, 10.0; .01 level of probability, 6.6).

Reports indicated that, among boys in the lower income group in New York, fighting occurred most often in response to aggression. Withdrawal was the most frequent response reported in cases of ridicule, physical ill-treatment, rude treatment, discrimination, and indirect disparagement. Low income girls fought in comparatively few instances, and only in response to physical ill-treatment or aggression. Withdrawal was the usual response in all other situations.

Upper income boys in New York fought most often in cases of aggression. Fighting was also a prevalent response in situations involving ridicule and physical ill-treatment. Withdrawal was complete in the remaining circumstances. Upper income girls fought most often in instances of physical ill-treatment and aggression, and argued in instances of ridicule. The dominating pattern, however, was that of withdrawal.

In St. Louis, socio-economic level again appeared to be unrelated to the frequency with which children in the two groups argued, fought, and withdrew. Fighting occurred only as a result of aggression, and withdrawal was the commonest response in all types of difficulties encountered for both boys and girls and in both income groups.

TABLE XV

PERCENTAGES OF CHILDREN REPORTING THE VARIOUS OVERT RESPONSES

| Type of Response | NEW YORK | | | | ST. LOUIS | | | |
| | Lower Income | | Upper Income | | Lower Income | | Upper Income | |
	B.	G.	B.	G.	B.	G.	B.	G.
Number of children reporting	30	30	15	15	15	15	15	15
Fought	30	13	53	27	40	13	20	0
Argued	13	17	7	33	20	33	20	27
Withdrew	73	90	60	67	67	80	87	93

Problem 4c

Is sex a factor related to the frequency of appearance of particular responses?

In the lower income group in New York, boys fought more often than girls. Girls withdrew more often. There was no significant difference in the amounts of arguing. In the upper income group in New York, boys again fought more often than girls, and there was no significant difference in the amounts of arguing and withdrawing. In St. Louis, sex was significant on one trait: upper income girls did no fighting.

Problem 5

Are children's overt responses indicative of what they felt like doing?

Table XVI presents the frequencies with which particular impulses of children are translated into the corresponding overt actions.

In New York, girls in the low income group reported a positive response in keeping with the nature of their impulses 22 per cent of the time. Lower income boys reported responding in the manner they desired 45 per cent of the time. Upper income boys carried through their impulses 54 per cent of the time, and upper income girls did so 29 per cent of the time.

TABLE XVI

Types of Impulses and Actual Responses, as Reported by All the Children

Type of Impulse	Frequency of Impulse	TYPE AND FREQUENCY OF RESPONSE	
		Fought or Argued	Accepted
To fight or argue	279	87	192
To accept	182	2	180
Unable to state what they felt like doing	26	0	26
Total	487	89	398

In St. Louis, lower income boys followed their impulses 32 per cent of the time, and low income girls did so 53 per cent of the time. Upper income boys responded as they desired in 16 per cent of the instances, and girls of this group did so in 10 per cent of the instances.

It appears from these data that some low income children who reported fewer aggressive impulses nevertheless activated or carried through their desires more often than did some upper income children.

Generally, it appears that expressions or response patterns may be distorted from their natural course if dominating attitudes or thought patterns are powerful enough to suppress them. The power of such attitudes as held by majority group members seems evident in the type of responses made by these children.

SUMMARY

Low income children were highly similar in kinds and frequencies of responses made. Irrespective of section, the immediate environment, which is a complex of family and group ideologies and boundaries of operation, is a potent directive of behavior. These children seem to have less opportunity for social communication with majority group members, probably because of their more restricted movements within their own group.

Upper income children in New York did more fighting than those in St. Louis. Two factors are suggested here. Protective civil rights measures of New York widen opportunity for participation, which in turn affects the thinking of the Negro about himself. These children may attempt to seek advantages of total community offerings and to retaliate when participation is threatened. The absence of such measures in St. Louis may be a factor in the greater amount of restraint witnessed there. Incidentally, upper income families in New York seem more aware of these measures than do lower income families.

Upper income girls in New York argued and fought more often than lower income girls, while in St. Louis no significant difference seemed to exist in the aggressiveness of the two groups.

Boys fought more often than girls and did so in response to ridicule, physical ill-treatment, and aggression.

Reports of all children indicate that they fought most often in response to physical ill-treatment and aggression, argued most often in reaction to ridicule, and withdrew most consistently in instances of rude treatment, discrimination, and indirect disparagement.

The difficulties reported represent an area of operation or an environment existing at a particular time. The responses made were a function of the possibilities of defense which that area offered at the moment. It is interesting to note the discrepancy between what children wanted to do, in relation to a particular problem, and what they actually did. Although a desire to fight was often felt in response to ridicule, the incidence of actual fighting in such cases was negligible; and although there was a desire to argue in cases of rude treatment and discrimination, there was in practice mainly withdrawal. If, however, in such instances in which the organism was geared for fighting and arguing a group rather than the individual had been present, fighting rather than withdrawal might have occurred. For example, shortly after the interviews were completed in St. Louis, a near riot was precipitated by an attempted conversion of a playground used by white children into one to be used by colored children. The setting embraced the low income district in which children reported relatively few attempts to strike back in comparison to the number of anger episodes reported. This kind of group behavior cannot be predicted with certainty, however, for the degree of influence of social controls will vary from one instance to another. It is nevertheless worthy of consideration when any attempt based on studies of individuals is made to label groups as aggressive or nonaggressive. It would be perhaps more valid to attempt prediction of the behavior of an individual in a particular setting than to label social groups as generally aggressive or nonaggressive.

A comparison of the extent of the desire to strike back with the overwhelming amount of withdrawal leads to the impression that emotions are associated with the withdrawal, and that such withdrawal cannot be inferred to be mere passive acceptance. A more likely inference is that internal rejection underlies the external acceptance based on a desire for personal security.

This lack of satisfying adjustive mechanism would point to a conflict between subjective attitudes and overt behavior. Further, it would indicate that restraint is more closely allied to social expectancies than to personal wants. Therefore, it appears that social controls reflecting caste have been internalized by children of this age—that such controls are operative as suppressive factors which interfere with satisfying adjustment. When such a condition prevails, there are probably inferiority feelings, resentments, and fears which interfere with wholesome personality development and effective functioning in the larger society.

The strength of these pressures in influencing personality development depends, of course, on the make-up of the particular person, and on the strength and effectiveness of other factors in the child's life development. Satisfactions may offset these difficulties. Children who expressed indifference to situations may have actually felt that way. It is true that negative adaption to pressures could have developed.

Chapter Six

SOCIAL PRESSURES IN RELATION TO
SKIN COLOR

Since the Negro population shows variation in skin color, it appeared appropriate to attempt to discover whether a relationship exists between skin color and the nature and frequency of pressures from the white world. This question must be distinguished from the question of in-group adjustment, for skin color has been found to influence social relationships and personal development within the Negro group. It is generally conceded that "evaluation of color and other physical traits made by Negroes themselves on their own group influence the development of personality." [1]

The children interviewed were classified into three skin color groups: light, medium, and dark. In the results as a whole, 26 per cent of the children were light and reported 21.1 per cent of the difficulties; 35 per cent were medium and reported 39.8 per cent of the difficulties; 39 per cent were dark and reported 38.3 per cent of the difficulties.

Criswell [2] noted in studying group cleavage in the classroom that "white children prefer light Negroes to medium and reject dark most." It appears from the present findings that in proportion to their number in the population, light children report fewer difficulties than medium and dark. The medium children in proportion to their number report more than light or dark. A possible consideration in accounting for the difference in the number reported by medium and dark children is that dark children may shy away from white individuals, and thus lessen their exposures to problems. This

[1] William L. Warner, *et al.*, *Color and Human Nature*. Washington, D. C., American Council on Education, 1941.

[2] Joan H. Criswell, *A Sociometric Study of Race Cleavage in the Classroom.* Archives of Psychology, No. 235. New York, Columbia University, 1939.

TABLE XVII

Percentages of Difficulties in the Various Categories Reported by Children
in a Given Skin Color Group

Skin Color	*Light*	*Medium*	*Dark*
Number of children reporting	39	52	59
Number of difficulties reported	106	194	187
Ridicule	26	29	30
Physical ill-treatment	4	2	7
Aggression	18	13	13
Rude treatment	7	7	6
Discrimination ....,.............,...	19	19	13
Indirect disparagement	26	30	29

in turn may be due to the possibility that derogatory reference to
dark color has been made in their presence by other Negroes, even
by family members, so that feelings of inferiority or insecurity
have become associated with dark skin. Thinking of this kind
may result in avoidance behavior.

Skin color differences and section

In New York, 23 per cent of the children were light and reported 18 per cent of the total number of difficulties; 32 per cent
were medium and reported 38 per cent; 44 per cent were dark and
reported 44 per cent. In St. Louis, 30 per cent of the children were
light and reported 26 per cent of the problems; 38 per cent were
medium and reported 42 per cent; 31 per cent were dark and reported 32 per cent. With respect to the number of difficulties
reported in each color group, the Chi-square test indicated no
significant differences between sections.

Skin color differences and income

There appears to be a relationship between color of skin and
socio-economic level, for the proportions in the light and dark sub-
groups tend to reverse themselves relative to income. In the lower
income group in New York, 9 per cent of the children were light
and 58 per cent dark. In the upper income group, 40 per cent of
the children were light and 17 per cent dark. A similar proportion
obtains in St. Louis. In the low income group 17 per cent of the

children were light and 53 per cent dark, while in the upper income group 43 per cent were light and 10 per cent dark. These results tend to agree rather closely with those of Warner[3] and his colleagues, who also examined color ranges in the economic groups.

When comparisons are made of the numbers of difficulties reported by children in the same color group but in contrasting socio-economic groups, differences do appear. Light and medium children in the upper income group reported more than light and medium children in the lower income group. The Chi-square value of 13.0 for light children and 11.0 for medium (.01 level of probability, 6.6) would indicate that differences in the distributions are significant. An extremely pronounced difference is seen in the dark group (Chi-square, 36.8; .01 level of probability, 6.6). Here the trend indicates that dark children in the low income group reported more difficulties than dark children in the upper income group.

Comparisons at a single economic level show that dark children reported 56 per cent of the total number of difficulties reported in the low income group. In the upper income group, 51 per cent of the difficulties were from children of medium skin color.

One cannot conclude from these findings, however, that color is a significant factor in relation to socio-economic level and difficulties reported because, as indicated in the statements above, there are more light and medium children at the upper income level, and more dark children at the lower level. When comparisons are made between the number of difficulties reported by light, lower income children and dark, upper income children, no significant differences appear.

Skin color differences and sex

Comparisons of frequencies of difficulties reported by each sex within each color group revealed no significant differences.

SUMMARY

In general, it appears from their reports that light children encounter fewer social pressures than medium and dark children, and

[3] Warner *et al., op. cit.,* p. 27.

may be preferred members of the group. Medium children tend to encounter more than the other two groups. These children may accept themselves with more assurance than dark group members, and may attempt to be more active in the larger world, thus exposing themselves to pressures through a larger number of contacts. As mentioned earlier, dark children may engage in more avoidance behavior.

Regional differences appear only in the dark group, children in New York reporting more difficulties than those in St. Louis.

The color of skin does not appear to be significantly related to socio-economic level and sex with reference to social pressures.

Chapter Seven

PARENTS' GUIDANCE AND RESPONSES TO HYPOTHETICAL SITUATIONS

Problem 6

What forms of guidance do parents provide?

According to the reports of children, 298, or 61 per cent, of the 487 difficulties experienced were reported to parents. In 13 per cent of these reported cases no guidance was given. The instruction most frequently received, appearing in 61 per cent of the instances, was to withdraw. That least often mentioned, appearing in 5 per cent of the cases, was to argue the point. (See Table XVIII.) Parents in general showed a rather clear tendency to discourage external conflict and to "keep the peace." No child stated that he had been given any a priori suggestions to follow or any forewarning which helped him in dealing with the circumstances attending intergroup relations. Incidentally, the question of proper timing in revealing to children the nature of the larger society is a major problem of the Negro parent, one on which there are two points of view. The first is that it is unwise to warn children ahead of time of experiences which they may encounter because of their group membership for this may develop a sensitivity and an undue consciousness of the self as different. The second point of view is that lack of this social knowledge results in an inadequate and unexpected meeting of the culture, with the child having developed no mechanism for lessening the impact of ego deflation. No real answer to this question has been given.

Problem 6a

Is kind of guidance given related to section?

As mentioned earlier, it appears that cultural expectancies dictate the extent of participation possible in a geographical setting. Recog-

TABLE XVIII

PERCENTAGES OF TYPES OF RESPONSE ADVISED IN PARENTS' GUIDANCE

Type of Response	Percentage of Instances in Which Advised (260)
Fight	7%
Argue	5
Withdraw	61
Avoid	26

nition by parents of the limiting aspects of these cultural demands possibly operates in selecting and determining the kinds of guidance children get. For example, parents in St. Louis recommended avoidance more often than those in New York (Chi-square, 12.3). Parents in New York advised withdrawal more often (Chi-square, 9.9; .01 level of probability in both instances, 6.6). Parents in St. Louis, aware of the prevalence of segregation patterns, may tend to restrict movement or tell children to avoid places and situations as a preventive measure. Parents in New York, in keeping with cultural patterns, may place less restraint on movement, but tend to emphasize withdrawal when social forces interfere with that movement.

Problem 6b

Is kind of guidance related to socio-economic level?

According to reports of children in both New York and St. Louis, socio-economic level was not related to frequency of instruction to fight or argue. In New York, socio-economic level was significant only in relation to avoidance guidance, which appeared more often in the upper income group (Chi-square, 26.2; .01 level of probability, 6.6). Since the kind of guidance given is relative, the types of experiences reported must be considered. Upper income children, as mentioned earlier, are probably more active in the total city setting, and thus report more situations involving intergroup contact. The same amount of activity on the part of lower income children might have resulted in as frequent avoidance guidance, or nearly so, by low income mothers. On the other hand, according

TABLE XIX

PERCENTAGES OF DIFFICULTIES AND TYPES OF RESPONSE ADVISED

	TYPE OF RESPONSE			
Type of Difficulty	*Fight* (18)	*Argue* (13)	*Withdraw* (159)	*Avoid* (70)
Ridicule	17	54	42	26
Physical ill-treatment	17	0	6	3
Aggression	66	15	16	27
Rude treatment	0	15	10	1
Discrimination	0	15	18	38
Indirect disparagement	0	0	8	4

to Johnson,[1] "avoidance . . . is most conspicuous in the efforts of upper class groups to preserve self-esteem." In the light of this statement it appears that this guidance was motivated by a conscious aim, and would occur more often in this group even if like situations appeared with the same frequency in low income groups.

Findings indicate that from 84 per cent to 94 per cent of the guidance in each income group was of the nature of withdrawal and avoidance. These, then, are the most prevalent types of counsel, cutting across all categories of difficulties regardless of the nature of the experience. The reason for this is not clear-cut. To tell the child to leave or avoid a situation rather than face it may, from the parent's point of view, be the path of least resistance. It might result from confusion with regard to the right response to make, or may represent a sincere belief prompted by fear of the consequences of other behavior.

As noted earlier, not all of the difficulties which children experienced were reported to their parents. According to reports of children, those in the lower income group in New York told parents about 59 per cent of the incidents which occurred, while those in St. Louis spoke about 56 per cent of them. Children in the upper income group in New York stated they reported 79 per cent of their experiences; those in St. Louis, 66 per cent. It appears that upper income children in both cities reported a substantially greater number of their experiences to parents than did lower income chil-

---

[1] Charles Johnson, *Patterns of Negro Segregation*. New York, Harper and Brothers, 1943.

dren (Chi-square, 10.7, New York; 10.2, St. Louis; .01 level of probability in both instances, 6.6).

The fact that lower income children speak of these problems less often may be due in part to family patterns. Mothers return home tired after a long working day, and have before them the evening meal to prepare and a variety of home chores to perform. Perhaps no more than the most cursory inquiry is made into the activities of the child's day. These children may early learn to shift for themselves and find their own answers to problems. When asked why they did not tell their mothers about the experiences mentioned, lower income children made such statements as these: "She might think I was in the wrong and get mad at me." "I just don't feel like telling her." "She wouldn't do nothing, no way." It is evident that a variety of factors influencing parent–child relationships are operating here. Degrees of confidence, sensed interest or lack of it on the part of parents, strength of family ties, and the unique make-up of the individual are facets of the pattern contributing to the behavior revealed.

Comparisons of the sets of frequencies with which reports were made to parents but no guidance was given showed again that low income children fared less well than upper income children (Chi-square, 9.7, New York; 33.0, St. Louis; .01 level of probability in both instances, 6.6). A statement repeatedly made by lower income children was, "She didn't say nothing when I told her." Upper income children reported such statements as: "Only mean people do that." "That wasn't nice of them." These responses were more in the nature of comments than of instruction. No upper income child reported that parents completely ignored the situation.

Problem 6c

Is kind of guidance given related to sex?

Some sex differences appear in relation to the nature of the guidance given. No lower income boy in New York reported avoidance counsel. In the upper income group, girls were told to withdraw more often (Chi-square, 11.7), and boys were told to avoid situations more often (Chi-square, 8.7; .01 level of probability in both instances, 6.6). In St. Louis, no lower income boy reported advice to argue. No upper income boy reported advice to fight.

In the lower and upper income groups in New York, and in the lower income group in St. Louis, no significant sex difference was found in the frequency of advice to fight back. Parents evidently associate fighting with self-defense, and those who advise it do so for boys and girls alike.

Summary

According to the reports of children, 39 per cent of their difficulties were not reported to parents. This report indicates that in situations involving intergroup conflict, as in other problems of daily living, children do not always seek the counsel of their parents. Reports of all children indicated withdrawal as the most frequently given advice, and retaliation through argument the least often given.

Although motivation for conduct is the same from region to region—preservation of self-esteem—the instruction designed to help the child achieve this end tends to differ with region. Regional variations in expected behavior patterns and in extent of Negro participation in the total life of a setting seem to influence the kind of guidance given. In New York the prevalent instruction was withdrawal; in St. Louis, avoidance.

There appears to be a relationship between the kind of guidance given and the responses to situations made by children. Withdrawal was the prevalent form of guidance, and also the prevalent response. The same kind of thinking evidently directs behavior of parents and children.

Socio-economic level is significant only in relation to avoidance guidance, which appears with greater frequency in the upper income group.

Economic level appears to be related to the frequency with which experiences are reported as well as to the frequency with which guidance is given.

Problem 7

Is parents' guidance effective, as judged by children?

In order to get some idea of the helpfulness of parental instruction in alleviating frustrations which result from racial conflicts, two questions were posed: (1) Is the guidance which parents give considered generally helpful by the children? (2) Which forms of guidance are most effective as judged by children?

Parental guidance may or may not result in satisfactory direction of behavior. Behavior which is satisfying to the individual helps him maintain a feeling of adequacy in the face of difficulty, and is repeated because of its effectiveness. Parental guidance is effective or ineffective depending upon its contribution to a feeling of personal adequacy in meeting these situations.

According to the reports of the children as a whole, 42 per cent of the guidance given was judged effective, and 48 per cent ineffective. In 10 per cent of the cases, children were unable to give any reactions to instructions received.

Reports indicated that in all instances in which children were told to fight back, this instruction was considered helpful. This was the only form of counsel in which there was perfect agreement by all the subjects. From the point of view of children, guidance of this nature—perhaps because it sanctioned a desire which might otherwise have caused guilt feelings, and because it suggested, at least, a positive attack on the problem—appears to have been the most helpful of the forms of instruction given.

In 55 per cent of the instances in which withdrawal guidance was given, children stated they did not consider the instruction helpful. Withdrawal guidance was least often reported as helpful, and would therefore appear to be the least effective in offsetting the negative feelings which accompany conflicts.

Generally, boys reported more often than girls that guidance was ineffective. (Chi-square, 10.6; .01 level of probability, 6.6.)

Problem 7a

Is effectiveness of guidance related to region?

It appears that children in St. Louis find instruction to avoid situations more helpful than do children in New York. In accounting, at least in part, for the difference, we may recall earlier findings which showed that children in St. Louis experience some confusion as to which business establishments they are permitted to enter for personal services. In addition, it was indicated that in this city discriminatory practices are pronounced. The distress which accompanies uncertainty in thinking and behavior may be relieved by advice which offers some measure of emotional security. Avoidance or circumvention of hurtful situations is thought of as a positive way to preserve a feeling of personal worth. In New York, however, as previously pointed out, thinking is not geared to the restriction of movement or to avoidance behavior. Children may thus think of advice to avoid particular settings as restrictive measures which are not compatible with their aspirations. They therefore report this advice as effective less often than St. Louis children do. (Chi-square, 12.6; .01 level of probability, 6.6.) This was the only significant regional difference observed.

Problem 7b
  Is effectiveness of guidance related to socio-economic level?

A difference in reported reactions to withdrawal guidance is very pronounced in the two income groups in New York. Lower income children reported this instruction as helpful more often than did upper income children. (Chi-square, 13.0; .01 level of probability, 6.6.) In the lower income group it was considered helpful 55 per cent of the time. In 15 per cent of the instances, children could not state whether it helped or not.

In the upper income group, guidance was reported effective 31 per cent of the time. In 11 per cent of the instances, children were unable to state reactions. In general, upper income children found instruction given less satisfying than did lower income children. (Chi-square, 8.8; .01 level of probability, 6.6.)

In St. Louis, a pronounced difference is again apparent in reactions to withdrawal guidance in the two income groups. Lower income children found it more satisfying than did upper income children. (Chi-square, 13.4; .01 level of probability, 6.6.) Low income girls in St. Louis showed a divergence from generally established group trends, in that none of them reported advice given as ineffective. Boys reported guidance helpful in but 20 per cent of the instances. In St. Louis, as in New York, upper income children found the kind of instruction given less effective in meeting problems than did the lower income group. (Chi-square, 13.5; .01 level of probability, 6.6.)

Summary

From the evidence available, it appears that parental instruction is not an extremely potent factor making for better ways of feeling, thinking, or acting; for guidance was reported helpful in but 42 per cent of the instances. It also appears improbable that, with the additional experiences which children will have in Negro–white relations, better ways of dealing with situations will follow; for a lack of satisfying guidance, which includes a lack of additional knowledge and lack of increasing skill in handling problems, tends to limit wise choice of behavior patterns.

Low income children in general and girls in both groups appear to be more receptive to counsel than other groups. A similar parallel in behavior of low income children and girls was pointed out earlier in the study. Boys and upper income children in general appear to be less susceptible and less satisfied with guidance given.

From these data it would seem that the Negro child in responding to social pressures is influenced in behavior choices most often by those social learnings which he acquires unaided, or with little aid from the home. It is possible, however, that a good deal of influence is exerted by way of example or of silence which is thought of as implying instruction.

GUIDANCE SUGGESTED BY PARENTS FOR HYPOTHETICAL SITUATIONS

Parents too were approached with reference to the kind of experiences reported to them by their children and the kinds of guidance given. Parents recalled an average of two experiences per person, but it was evident from the outset that it would be difficult to secure accuracy in reporting. Terms too vague for precision were often used. For example, parents would say, "He has told me about being called nigger by white people," or "They get into fights sometimes." Any statement of the actual number of instances of name-calling or of fighting, however, was at best a hazardous guess. It therefore appeared feasible to use the interview opportunity to better advantage by projecting hypothetical situations and eliciting the parents' basic and pervasive attitudes.

Two factors arise which should be considered in relation to responses of parents. First, practically en masse, regardless of training or background, parents stated that they really did not know what to say to their children when reports of this type were made to them. Those whose children had reported no experiences were at an even greater loss to give any directives. The responses made to these hypothetical situations may, therefore, be mainly gropings in the dark, and there is no assurance that such statements actually foretell behavior in future situations. Nevertheless the sincerity with which parents presented what they considered the best advice seems worthy of attention because it does reveal current attitudes toward adjustment in Negro–white relations. The responses of parents in these hypothetical situations are set forth and comparisons made on the basis of section, socio-economic level, and skin color.

In the responses as a whole, all four types of advice (to fight, to argue, to withdraw, and to ignore) were included in the statements of all parents irrespective of region, socio-economic level, or skin color. Instructions to withdraw were given most often and appeared in 41 per cent of the instances. Other responses following in the order of frequency were: to ignore, 16 per cent; to fight back, 15 per cent; to argue back, 10 per cent; to seek legal redress, 3 per cent; to explain worth of self, 3 per cent; to report all instances to parents and let them handle the situation (complete identification of parent with child's difficulty), 2 per cent. In 12 per cent of the instances, parents were unable to make a statement.

Relation between section and guidance suggested
for hypothetical situations

One type of guidance suggested by New York parents was reference to use of legal redress when faced with violation of civil rights. This of course was not mentioned by parents in St. Louis. Included in the forms mentioned in St. Louis but not in New York were instructions to report all conflicts and let parents intercede and handle the situations completely. No significant regional differences were found relative to the frequency with which fighting, arguing, withdrawing, or ignoring was recommended.

*Relation between socio-economic level and guidance
suggested for hypothetical situations*

Lower income mothers in both cities were somewhat less ingenious than upper income mothers in devising different forms of guidance. While low income mothers in St. Louis and New York recommended four and five possible behavior patterns respectively, upper income parents in the two cities mentioned six and seven. In New York at the low income level there was no mention of avoidance or reference to civil rights laws. Another example of contrast in thinking at the two levels in this city is seen in guidance recommended in situations involving ridicule. While 18 per cent of the low income mothers advised fighting, no upper income mother suggested it; and while 17 per cent of the low income mothers mentioned withdrawal in relation to ridicule, no upper income mother referred to it as an adjustment aid.

In relation to situations involving aggression, no significant difference was apparent in the amount of fighting back recommended by upper and lower income parents. However, a factor not readily measurable was discernible. This is concerned with the readiness with which fighting is advocated in the two groups. Upper income mothers were reluctant to mention it, stating that only as a practical defense measure and last resort should children turn to it. The lower income mothers who mentioned it stated, with gusto and without hesitation, that one must fight back. In other words, when this group of mothers did mention it they were quite positive. However, the parents who advocated aggressive measures were not in the majority in either group. In the lower income group members were loud in their admonitions to children to "keep the peace" and not make trouble. Typical responses were: "Don't fight back because then you will get the parents into it, and you might start a race riot." "Don't pay any attention to what they do." "Be nice to them."

As shown in Table XX, 55 per cent of these parents were from Southern states, 28 per cent from the West Indies. The remaining 17 per cent were born in Northern states. The place of birth of the parent did not seem significantly related to the type of guidance recommended by members of the low income group. Parents from

TABLE XX

BIRTHPLACE OF NEW YORK PARENTS INTERVIEWED AND NUMBER OF YEARS'
RESIDENCE IN NEW YORK

Birthplace	NUMBER OF YEARS IN NEW YORK								PROPORTION OF TOTAL	
	Less than 5		5–10		10–15		Over 15			
	L.*	U.*	L.	U.	L.	U.	L.	U.	L.	U.
South	6	0	6	3	12	4	9	3	55	33
West Indies	0	0	1	0	5	0	11	0	28	0
North	0	0	0	0	5	0	5	20	17	67
Total	6	0	7	3	23	4	25	23	100	100

* L = Lower income group, U = Upper income group, in all tables.

TABLE XXI

BIRTHPLACE OF ST. LOUIS PARENTS INTERVIEWED AND NUMBER OF YEARS'
RESIDENCE IN ST. LOUIS

Birthplace	NUMBER OF YEARS IN ST. LOUIS								PROPORTION OF TOTAL	
	Less than 5		5–10		10–15		Over 15			
	L.	U.	L.	U.	L.	U.	L.	U.	L.	U.
South	8	0	6	4	5	6	0	0	63	33
Mid-West	0	0	0	0	0	0	9	14	30	47
North	0	0	0	0	2	5	0	1	7	20
Total	8	0	6	4	7	11	9	15	100	100

the West Indies, however, showed a contrast in the certainty and conviction with which they held an idea. A seeming feeling of superiority over the American Negro, borne out of a background which did not embrace servitude to the white man, perhaps caused these individuals to speak with less hesitancy about right and wrong. Southern-born parents, on the other hand, seemed confused by the strong resentments of children, for these conflicted with conceptions of caste discipline which the parents had retained. For example, one mother from Alabama said, "The colored children go in the store on the corner and yell at the white man and say, 'Hey, Benjamin, give me some milk.' I always correct my kids. I say,

'Always call him Mister. Don't go talking to him like you are talking to another kid. You just make trouble.' Of course, my children get mad, and they're always fussing when I tell them how to act. They say the white folks treat 'em bad, and they always razz 'em. Of course, I don't mind staying in my place."

A parent from Georgia said, "New York is worse than the South. Up here you don't know what to expect. Down there you know you can't go some places, and you know just what to do; but up here you don't, and you can get into trouble. There ain't nothing you can do about it nowhere, I guess. I guess you just have to ignore everything. That's why, when white children call my children names and want to fight, I just tell 'em to come on away and don't do nothin'. There ain't nothing they can do. I just don't know what else to say."

As earlier stated, the dominant kind of advice given by mothers in both groups in relation to aggression was withdrawal, and there was no significant difference in the frequency with which it appeared in the two groups.

While 23 per cent of the low income mothers stated that children should argue their way into a setting, such as a public building or playground, when discriminated against, no upper income mother advocated this behavior. Rather, 47 per cent of them advocated use of civil laws as protective weapons. That this weapon may have lucrative returns is illustrated by one upper income mother who stated that daughters of some of the better known residents of Harlem seasonally acquired entire new wardrobes by entering restaurants, operated by a well-known syndicate, in which they knew they would be refused. They had learned all the directives to follow whereby they could promptly and successfully sue the establishment. The mother added that the establishment after many seasons finally "caught on" to the well-planned operations, so that now service is given to Negroes without delay. No lower income mother mentioned this technique.

Advice to withdraw was mentioned with the same frequency in both groups.

In St. Louis, as in New York, both upper and lower income mothers advised fighting only in relation to aggression. Upper income mothers again mentioned it, not as an expression of hostility, but as a defense measure. Upper income mothers also included in their guidance the suggestion to explain one's worth and importance. This is best achieved, it was thought, through quoting short, pointed "stock phrases." These mothers also mentioned parental intercession—children to report all experiences but do nothing themselves. Neither of these forms was mentioned by low income mothers.

Relation between skin color and guidance suggested
for hypothetical situations

During the interviews close attention was paid to the skin color of the person reporting. Of the sixty low income parents interviewed in New York, 1 was white, 12 per cent were light, 30 per cent medium, and 57 per cent dark in skin color. In response to questions asked, the one white parent, mother of four girls, appeared quite bewildered and stated that it had never occurred to her that her children would meet such problems. Her concern was that of getting the colored children to accept her girls, who she said were rejected because of their white mother. Incidentally, no white fathers were observed in the group, but four white grandfathers were members of households. One dark-skinned mother completely denied Negro ancestry, and said her family were Black Jews. However, since the mother admitted that they were treated as Negroes in the larger society, her interview report was included with the others.

In the lower income group in New York it appeared that skin color was unrelated to the kind of guidance indicated in responses to hypothetical situations. The largest number of parents, 44 per cent, advised withdrawal, and the smallest, 1 per cent, suggested that a comment be given which would tend to point up the child's worth or importance.

In the upper income group in New York, the color distribution was as follows: light, 53 per cent; medium, 33 per cent; dark, 13 per cent. The light-skinned mothers were the only ones in this group to state that children should argue back and should tell white individuals of their worth. This advice was given in relation to ridicule in 44 per cent of the instances. With this exception, skin color seemed to be unrelated to kinds of guidance given.

In the lower income group in St. Louis, skin color was found in the following proportions: light, 17 per cent; medium, 30 per cent; dark, 53 per cent. No skin color factor was apparent in relation to the frequency with which a particular kind of guidance was given.

In the upper income group in St. Louis, 57 per cent of the parents were light in color; 37 per cent, medium; and 6 per cent, dark. Again, no skin color differences were found. The only differences were noted in relation to counsel in situations of discrimination and ridicule. Light mothers were the only ones to mention arguing with reference to discrimination, and parental intercession with reference to ridicule.

Summary

Responses in general to hypothetical situations indicate greater similarity than difference between groups. "Fight," "argue," "withdraw," and "ignore" were the major forms of behavior advised, and these were mentioned by mothers irrespective of region, socioeconomic level, and skin color. This might indicate that responses represent basic thought patterns that can only be ascribed to human reactions to a common pattern. Further, it may show that responses to such problems involve emotion as well as reason, and that intellect may not be the most potent factor operating. Subjective feelings immersed in parent–child relationships may be attached to directives given.

The slight variation noted in the number of different directives given, however, would indicate that upper income mothers have developed more approaches which possibly grow out of more strategic philosophies and thinking.

PARENTS' RESPONSES TO RELATED QUESTIONS

In an attempt to explore attitudes further and to obtain an understanding of the backgrounds of these attitudes, questions as well as hypothetical situations were presented.

It is assumed that participation in intergroup activities which aim at bettering race relations might have some influence on the thinking of, and subsequently the guidance given by, parents. To this end, inquiry was made as to membership in intergroup organizations, and as to the effectiveness of such activities. Mothers in the low income group in New York reported practically no experiences of this nature. One mother mentioned the presence of white members in the church which she attended; two spoke of having attended meetings with white people on matters pertaining to school problems. Only one individual spoke of a meeting which appeared in the aspect of a true intergroup activity. The majority of them could refer only to election activities, at which time candidates for office campaigned in Negro districts and brought other white persons with them.

Responses, then, with reference to the effectiveness of such organizations are not based, in the majority of cases, on reactions to real experiences. The reactions of the mothers to these proposed interracial groups were as follows: 20 per cent stated that meetings were probably helpful; 38 per cent stated that they were not helpful; and 33 per cent felt that they could not answer the question because they knew nothing about such groups. Of those who thought the meetings might be helpful, the largest percentage in proportion to their number in the group were light in skin color. Of those rejecting them as not helpful, the largest percentage were dark.

The general attitudes of those who did not think meetings of this sort were of much use are reflected in these typical statements: "Interracial groups ain't so good. White people talk nice in front of your face, but what they say behind your back! Those meetings don't mean nothing." "I don't think they do any good. It's like a cat and a dog being in a room together and getting along all right while they are there, but as soon as the dog gets out of the room he starts tearing out after all the cats. Behind your back you can't trust them." A lack of belief in the sincerity of white group members seemed to characterize the thinking.

Another question proposed was related to attitudes toward segregation. It is hypothesized that attitudes toward intermixing in public places might have some effect on the guidance given in cases of discrimination. The question was therefore asked, "Do you think white people are justified in demanding segregation?" In response, 28 per cent of the lower income mothers stated that segregation was agreeable to them. The following are typical statements:

"Segregation is all right with me. Colored people need to be alone. White people think they are better than Negroes so it is just better to stay away from them." "It's all right with me. It don't bother me none." "My honest opinion is, segregation gives the Negro a chance to get up in the world and do for themselves. They ought to have their own businesses." "I'm from the South; I'm used to segregation. I think it's all right when colored people have places separate from white people. They get along better." Of those stating that segregation was agreeable to them, the largest percentage in proportion to their number in the group were dark in skin color. Of those rejecting segregation, the largest percentage were light in skin color.

Another question dealt with the effectiveness of churches in helping in Negro–white adjustments. According to the reports of 90 per cent of these parents, churches are not active in any program which tends to better intergroup relations.

Answers of low income mothers to a question about what approaches might be helpful if activated are listed below. It will be noted that one of the two largest groups stated that nothing would help, and the other group said they didn't know what would be really helpful.

Answer	*Number Answering*
Nothing	13
Don't know	12
Working together	8
Better Negro leaders	6
Church activities; knowledge of God	5
Education of white persons	2
Less aggression by Negroes	2
More mixing in schools	2
Active parent–teacher associations	2
Teaching of love, patience, and tolerance by parents	2
Fight it out	2
Intermarriage	2
Holding projects, Negro–white together	2

In the upper income group in New York, reactions to intergroup meetings indicated that the majority of parents favored them: 93 per cent stated they were effective and should be encouraged. All of the parents rejected the idea of segregation. Two stated they could understand why some Negroes would subscribe to it, however, because of their background. Churches were considered ineffective by 73 per cent of these parents. Activities mentioned as things that are or might be done to improve relationships are listed below.

Activity	*Number Mentioning*
Early rich, integrated or intergroup, life experiences sponsored by Y.M.C.A. and Y.W.C.A., camps, social and civic groups..	20
Better-planned action by Negroes, embracing adult education study groups	7
Functional educational surveys of what is happening; exposures to enlighten population	3

In the low income group in St. Louis, the parents were less like-minded than those of New York on the subject of the good inherent in intergroup enterprises: 46 per cent favored them; 40 per cent rejected them; and 14 per cent didn't know anything about them. In general, these parents seemed better acquainted with such meetings and were less vehement than the similar group in New York in their rejection of them. In relation to segregation, 40 per cent of the parents accepted it because it lessened chances of embarrassment in public places, and 56 per cent rejected it. A majority—63 per cent—of these parents were from Mississippi, Oklahoma, and South Carolina, where segregation had always been a part of their life. Churches are considered ineffective by 73 per cent of the parents.

Answers to the question about what is helpful in improving relations follow:

Answer	*Number Answering*
Don't know	5
Equal rights and opportunity for freedom	5
Nothing	4
Improvement of Negroes depends upon themselves	4
Church	4
Growing up together	3
Negroes respect each other	3
Don't agitate	1
Patience through time	1

Of the upper income mothers, 80 per cent felt that some good resulted from interracial groups. However, there were those who felt that such groups had not reached the point of greatest effectiveness. A majority—75 per cent—rejected segregation, while the remainder could see some advantages in it for the Negro in business or the professions. The farther south one goes, the more numerous are Negro business enterprises. Fewer of the upper income parents in St. Louis than of those in New York rejected the idea of segregation. Only 30 per cent of these parents felt that churches were effective.

The following are ways suggested by the upper income St. Louis mothers for bettering relations:

Suggestion	*Number Suggesting*
Mixed schools	11
Negro parents make children better advertisements for group	6
Better training of white children	4
Better economic conditions and opportunities	4
Lift ban on segregation	1
Churches	1
Improvement of conduct by Negroes	3

REACTIONS OF LOW INCOME CHILDREN AND PARENTS TO WHITE TEACHERS

Although originally the study was not designed to deal with schools, the investigator was soon aware from unsolicited statements of children and parents in the low income group in New York that the school was a cause for concern. It appeared feasible, therefore, to retain such data as was given, and to make a systematic inquiry along the lines suggested.

As suggested earlier, the circumscribed physical nature of lower West Harlem places definite limitations on the acquaintance which the low income Negro child has with the white world. Systematic face-to-face contacts are afforded in large measure through the teacher, the policeman, and tradespeople—mainly individuals in authoritarian roles.

Table XXII presents the number of difficulties reported by these children, and the sources of the difficulties as revealed by the questions asked.

TABLE XXII

NUMBER OF DIFFICULTIES REPORTED IN RESPONSE TO QUESTIONS ASKED

Question	Boys	Girls	Total
Do you ever have quarrels, misunderstandings, fights, with other children? Are these colored or white children or both? Etc.	19	25	44
Have white children ever made fun of you? What did they say? Etc.	8	16	24
Do you have a white teacher or a colored teacher? Is she nice to the class? Is she nice to you? Etc.	11	30	41
Do you ever have trouble with the grocer, butcher, bakery man, or candy store man? Tell me about it.	2	6	8
Have you ever been turned away from the park, playground, museum, or any place where other people go? What happened?	2	2	4
Do you ever go to the movies? What do you think about the movies with Negro characters?	21	35	56
Have you ever gone in an all white neighborhood? How did you feel? What happened?	1	4	5
Total	64	118	182

Difficulties in classroom situations fell under the categories of ridicule (including name calling), disparagement, physical ill-treatment, and rude treatment. Illustrative of classroom conflicts are the following accounts:

"I think the teachers are prejudiced, but the children act bad too. One teacher sure made me feel bad. When you go up to his desk and ask him a question, he says, 'Stay back there. Stay back there when you want to ask a question.' He wants to keep you at a distance. Then I've seen him put his arm around somebody, then take it away and brush his sleeve off."

"Last semester the teacher I had was fussing and she forgot and almost called a girl black (you could tell what she was going to say); then she changed off and said something else. She was terrible. She hollered and screamed at us and called us deaf, and said we didn't have no sense. She even called us worms and snakes and said we had gnats in our backsides."

"I have a white teacher. She's mean. She gives you thirty seconds to do hard arithmetic, and if you don't get it she slaps you in the face with a ruler."

Some illustrations of parent reports follow:

"Bobbie came home one day and said the teacher got mad at one of the boys and called him a nigger. I guess she forgot."

"One day my child came home from school and told me that the teacher took them to the zoo; and when they came to the monkey cage, she said, 'That's where you colored children come from.' They knew she was making fun of them."

"He's had terrible treatment at school. One day the teacher hit him so hard in the jaw he couldn't eat. Another day he came home with both eyes swollen where she had hit him."

Such extremes in the behavior of some white teachers, as illustrated above, would seem to reflect an ideology of domination as a classroom requisite, and to point to instances wherein teachers have not adjusted to life problems and have seemingly garnered instead a defense of hostility toward the situations they would like to reject.

In the light of reports of children and parents with reference to school conflicts, it appeared feasible to attempt to get the reaction of parents to white individuals teaching Negro children. In the lower income group, 70 per cent of the parents favored Negro teachers. In the upper income group, 70 per cent of the parents stated that more Negro teachers should be employed, but none stated that there should be complete elimination of white teachers, as some low income parents did.

Upper income children tended to live in districts or to attend schools where the Negro membership was small. These children and parents reported no classroom conflicts which were directly attributed to the fact that they were Negro.

ILLUSTRATIONS OF INTERVIEWS

In order to see the foregoing discussion in its living context, insofar as possible, and to allow to some extent a synthesis of the analysis made, three of the interviews are presented below.

I

Muriel, eleven years old, unlike most of the other low income children interviewed, attended a parochial school. She appeared eager and anxious to talk, but an occasional sigh and a wistful note in voice tone tended to give the impression that there was either indulgence in self-pity or a mature concern for the gravity of pressing problems. The interview languished when an older sister came in, and Muriel left the room soon afterward. The following is her account of her experiences:

When I first went to the Catholic school, the children called me blackie and nigger. It made me feel just awful. I felt like getting them and tearing them to bits, like paper. [Tearing motion demonstrated.] At first I didn't do nothing; then my mother said, "Call them old white trash." When I did that, they went and told the Sister, and they added a story to it. The Sister told me it was wrong to say that. She got after me, so it didn't help me none to say anything.

My mother used always to give me nice clean uniforms to wear. My blouse was always clean and white and I had a change of skirts. Some of the white children had dirty clothes on, and I didn't like to play with them. Then they started picking fights with me.

They'd chase me home. I didn't know how to fight, but some colored children around here showed me how. I don't fight so well now, but when they hit me, I try to hit them back. My mother said to hit them back.

At first, there were two of us in my room. I started when I was in the fourth grade. Now I'm in the sixth grade and there are twelve colored children in my room, and six Spanish and two Puerto Ricans; and the rest are Irish. There are forty-eight in the room altogether.

The Fathers don't say nothing to us colored children. One day one of the Fathers was taking pictures of the school children. I went up and asked him to take mine. He said he didn't have no more films, and he wouldn't take mine. I really think he didn't want to take colored children's pictures. I felt bad because I really wanted to have my picture taken. My mother happened to be passing going to work and she saw what happened. She said I shouldn't have asked him after the other colored girl did, and he didn't take hers.

They have plays at my school a lot, but I don't have no main part. I'm always in the chorus. At Christmas time, I was one of the Wise Men. In the plays they pick children according to what they look like. I don't like it. I don't do nothing about it. Once I went over to New Jersey with my mother and we went in a restaurant to eat. They kept us waiting and waiting. White people came in after us and they waited on them. My mother asked the waiter, "Don't you serve this table too?" She said real mean and loud, "When I get to it." She never did wait on us, and nobody else came over. We had to leave. I felt real embarrassed going out. Mama said she guessed that was just the way they were over in New Jersey. I didn't want to go back there. I don't go no place much because I don't want to be turned away.

I don't go to the movies much. I saw Lena Horne once when my mother took me. I like her, but I didn't like the colored people in "Caldonia." It was a colored orchestra. I just didn't like them at all. I was glad when it was over. It made colored people look too rough.

I don't like colored people on the radio. I don't like the way they sound. It doesn't make me feel good. I turn it off. I listen to the stories. I like murder stories. I listen to Inner Sanctum. Sometimes I get awfully scared if I'm here by myself, and I just sweat all over, but after that, I turn on Fibber McGee or something like that and try to make myself happy.

I don't have any friends. Don't no children come to see me. I play with my dolls. I take them on trips and play school. I'm happy when I play with them.

I wouldn't like to go in a neighborhood with just white people in it by myself. I wouldn't mind it if somebody was with me so I'd have someone to talk to. I go to Mass, but the priest doesn't say anything about white people and colored people getting along together. I think white people just don't like us.

The substance of the interview with Muriel's mother lends some support to the belief that Muriel is enmeshed in a pattern in which she probably justifiably feels some social rejection by both Negroes and white persons. Color of skin may be associated as a factor in the rejection. It would appear that negative thinking on the child's part might develop a "turned-in" personality which in turn might make for poor adjustment. The mother's report follows:

Muriel has told me from time to time about things that happened to her in school. I just don't understand why the children treat her like they do. She was a nice soft kind of child when she started to this school, and she didn't know how to be rough. She's darker than my other children and her hair just won't grow, but she always looks nice. I guess I spend more on her clothes than some of the other children's parents. She always looks neat and clean, but the children pick on her and call her nigger.

When they have plays over there, Muriel says they pick the children according to what they look like. I guess because they have religious plays with the Virgin Mary and things like that they don't want to give colored children any main parts. Muriel says they always put her in the chorus.

If they wanted her to play a slave girl, I'd tell her not to do it. It develops an inferiority complex. You have to make children think they are as good as the next one.

One day I came home and Muriel was crying, and she was just nine years old. She said she was going to kill herself, and was awfully upset.

She said she did something at school, and the teacher told her she wasn't no good and her mother knew it and just dressed her up trying to make something out of her.

You see, when my husband died, I was expecting a child in three months, and I didn't have but three dollars to my name. We married young, and were just struggling along. I didn't have money even to bury him, and no insurance. We already had three children; and on top of this, there was a big furniture bill because we did have a nice home. I was just desperate. My family had to chip in and bury my husband. My mother stayed here with me about a year after the child was born, then she went back to the West Indies and took the children with her until I could get myself going with a job and everything. I was thinking that maybe I could make a better home for the children if I got married. I was beginning to get along pretty good, but when I started trying to get married, that was my downfall. It was just unfortunate because Muriel was born and I wasn't married. It was just a stumbling block.

Just at that time something happened at home and my mother had to send the children to me. Well, the children knew their father was dead and that I wasn't married, and they just didn't like Muriel. They never have been nice to her. She doesn't look like the rest of the children. Their father was light and his children are all much lighter than Muriel and they have nice hair.

I told them about Muriel when I was trying to get her in the Catholic school. I wanted her to have a chance. Maybe they just don't think she's anything, either. I don't know what to do. She won't talk to us half the time. Sometimes I think it would be better to send her to a boarding school, but I just don't know what to do.

Even the colored children of the nice type don't play with her. There are some that are rough that she plays with some time, but it worries me. I don't think they are the right kind so I don't have them come around. Muriel doesn't have any friends at all.

When the school children call her names, I tell her to call them names right back. I condemn the white people. I tell her they are just ignorant.

They used to fight her. I think she'll try to fight back now; that's all there is to do.

If she's turned away from any place, I just tell her that you have to get accustomed to it; it's just ignorance. We are people just like they are.

Of course, in stores and things, our children act bad a lot of times, and they're in the wrong. They bring trouble on themselves.

Sometimes I think segregation, having your own schools and churches like that might be better, people might be more interested in you, but after all, it doesn't help us go forward. I guess we should try to make no sudden changes right now. We'll have to wean away from things gradually. We just have to wait, watch, and pray.

I belong to this Catholic church on the corner, and as long as I've been a member, nobody has said one word to me. They are almost all Irish. They are not at all friendly.

Interracial groups aren't active among adults. They could do some good, but I really don't think white people are sincere.

I don't know what would help Negro and white people get along better together; I thought you could do it through education, but I don't think you can.

II

Mary, twelve years old, a low income girl, appears to have developed some independence in building a defense, for herself and her group membership, based upon her conception of man's origin through God. Thus she not only justifies her appearance, but also extols a great group loyalty because God has so ordained her role. Her report is as follows:

I play with the boys and girls at school, and we get along like that together. [Indicates by putting two fingers together.]

I see white children lots of times. I see them in the store on the corner. The little ones try to act smart, but I get along with the big ones. The little ones lick out their tongue and call you nigger and things like that. I just don't pay them no mind. I feel like doing something. Inside I feel terrible, but I don't do nothing because it won't do no good. If you start fighting then you'll get all beat up, and it will just make things worst. You'll be fighting all the time. The older children know better how to act. They are sometimes better than the colored children because they don't fight so much. I don't bother to tell my mother; it happens too much. You know I don't like for the white children to call me black or anything like that because God made me this way. He meant for me to be brown, and for them to be white, but they ain't no better than me. I'm black and I know it, but I don't mind it. I'm proud of it. My mother tells me not to fight about what they do, so I just pass them up, but I don't like it, because God wanted me to be this way.

I see colored people in the show playing maids and servants, and I don't like that at all. They are all blacker than colored people really are. I don't like that. Colored people don't look that way. It makes me feel like colored people have to be slaving for white people. There's nothing I can do about it though. What can I do?

I don't like some of the radio parts either. They are the same old thing. The colored people have to bust suds, and the white people are so precious—so much better than you are. But remember I don't mind being colored.

I went to the museum once and the colored children were in one part and the white children were off to themselves. I don't mean in all of the museums.

Our teacher was all right I guess, but to tell the truth, she didn't like but three of us. I guess it was because the children acted so bad. She was nice. I don't know who my teacher will be when we go back.

I went up to Morningside Avenue, then up to the steps to the street up there. I just go when I am clean because I know the white people will talk about you if you are not clean, and it will make the whole race look bad. I'll tell you something else. When we were going to South Carolina they made us change coaches in Washington. I felt so bad, and I got real mad. I wanted to tell them a whole lot, to bawl them out. It sure did make me mad to have to move up there just because I was colored. I started talking about it. My mother wanted me to stop saying anything. She told me to shut up—that I was talking too loud. I couldn't do nothing but go on in there. Like in the museum. It made me feel like we were so separated. Like we are so different. But I know that I'm just as good. No, what my mother says to me doesn't help. They don't tell us nothing [in Sunday school] about how to get along with white people. Of course, I haven't been there much.

I haven't been turned away from any place yet, but I won't be surprised because white people just don't want you around.

III

Stewart, ten years old, low income New York boy whose mother has little contact with him because of long working hours, expresses a spirit of aggression born perhaps out of the necessity of fending for himself in the wider environment. His report follows:

I go up to the park on Morningside Avenue. When white children are there they get up on the stones and call us dirty names, and throw sharp rocks. A white boy called my mother a black so-and-so. I jumped up and busted him one. I started running then 'cause the cops might have come. They are always calling me names like blackie and nigger. They always act like they are better than you. If I could catch them I sure would take 'em and beat 'em. I'd kill them. They are just against Negroes. It makes me real mad. They start it, and I fight 'em back. Sure my mama know it. Sometimes she don't say nothing; then sometimes she say, "Beat 'em up if they bother you. Kill 'em." My mama don't have to tell me nothing about those old white boys. I'll beat 'em dead.

Sure colored kids call me names, but they just playing.

Another thing about white children. I don't like to be around them because they try to rule you. When they try to rule me I stay away from them. Then, it's hard to know how to call their names. They think they are more than colored children. That's just the way the cops are. When the colored cops are with the white, they try to be white. When they are just with colored people, they try to rule them. The white cops don't bother you.

I don't like the teacher. She's mean,—mean! I didn't like the last one either. She was mean too. They are both white. Aw, I don't know how I felt. I don't know what I felt like doing except to tell her something. I don't do nothing. There ain't nothing I can do.

I don't like the storeman on the corner. I went to help a boy who is my friend take out some orders. The man was always counting things over and over and saying things to us like we was going to steal something. He made me real mad. I felt like telling him I wasn't going to steal none of his old stuff. He sent a lady some cola and he kept counting it and telling us about it. I wasn't working for him. I was trying to help out my friend. There's a bunch of us. We stick together. I stopped going around there, though. He didn't treat the white boy that way.

I don't like the way colored people look in the movies. They make 'em black, as black as a blackboard with big old thick lips. Sometimes they got on raggedy clothes. The white people look nice. It makes me mad. I don't know what I feel like doing. What can you do?

Naw, I ain't been in a white neighborhood. I don't want to go.

I ain't never heard them say nothing about white people in Sunday school, 'cause I don't go much.

Chapter Eight

SUMMARY AND CONCLUSIONS

THE basic purpose of this study was to investigate the problems, fears, annoyances, frustrations, and other emotional difficulties common to Negro children because of the fact that they are Negro. Information about the following pertinent related matters was also sought: the influence of these experiences on feeling tones, inner impulses, and overt responses; the kinds of guidance given by parents, and the effectiveness of the guidance; and the attitudes of parents, toward certain existing social conditions, which might influence the kind of guidance given.

The group interviewed consisted of seventy-five girls and seventy-five boys, ranging in age from ten to twelve years, and representing contrasting socio-economic levels as determined by occupational status and cultural background of parents. Ninety children lived in New York City, and sixty in St. Louis. One hundred and fifty parents representing contrasting socio-economic levels in the regions mentioned were also included.

The interview method was used because it appeared to be the best technique available, at the time, for obtaining the information needed.

CONCLUSIONS AND INTERPRETATIONS

An indication of social direction at a given time may be obtained through a study of what is happening to the children of a culture. An adequate concept of American culture must recognize the thoughts and behavior of growing Negro children who are products of, and thus reflectors of, that culture.

The seeming fact that the Negro child perceives clues which enable him to attach significance to himself as different, and early learns to limit his expectations of freedom of movement and gratification of desires in the larger society, indicates that social controls are present and operative. The fact that these social pressures transcend selective factors such as geographical location, socioeconomic level, and skin color of individuals indicates that they are widespread and no respecter of persons. The fact that Negro children overtly respond, in most instances, in like manner to these pressures may indicate that, irrespective of the individual security systems that have been built, the force of social pressures is dynamic enough to result in behavior more reflective of these modifying social controls than of the unique individuality of the child. The behavior shown may thus be thought of as a culturally determined phenomenon rather than a characteristic pattern—an enactment of a cultural role as the culture is interpreted by the child.

Although the impulse overwhelmingly reported by children was to strike back, true reactions were usually concealed by adherence to social expectancies and the most prevalent response was withdrawal. Fear may cause the individual child to respond by withdrawing from a situation. However, suppressed hostility may find expression later in group action. The form of expression which social tendencies take depends upon the interplay of all the forces operating in the field at a given time.

It appears that the Negro child tends more toward the suppression of emotions, and withdrawal, when difficulties of the nature explored are encountered, than he does toward the active seeking of devious routes to circumvent the barriers. This, however, may be due to the fact that difficulties encountered are so deep-seated, unpredictable as to appearance, and protected that withdrawal may be the best possible adjustment he can make or knows how to make.

Social pressures or stresses of the nature recorded serve as obstructions to satisfaction of the vital needs of social acceptance, belongingness, and security. Frustration emerges as a result of threats to ego-striving and affects the personality as a whole. It is possible that lack of satisfying mechanisms of adjustment in early stages of life may instill unsatisfactory patterns of reaction which persist through time, and limit the individual's ability to react adequately in later situations. Negro children may develop enduring inferiority feelings which pervade all avenues of development, lowering aspiration levels and stifling individual abilities. It would appear that more can be learned of the nature of pressures by observing their effects over a period of time than by observing the immediate response made to them by individuals.

Cultural difficulties met during childhood may, if they remain unsolved, result in disturbed adults who are unable to participate effectively in the larger society or contribute to its growth.

Social factors which lead to disorganization in the life of the Negro child reflect the antisocial attitudes of individuals. It would seem, then, that significant trends in social betterment are contingent upon reconstructed thought patterns.

Numerical accounting shows no significant differences between income groups and skin color groups among parents in relation to the kinds of guidance given. However, motivation behind specific directives may vary. The reactions of Southern-born parents and lower income parents indicate greater fear of social penalties, and a desire for peace at any price. Northern-born and upper income parents are more concerned with preserving the wholeness of the personality structure.

In general, it appears that guidance in Negro–white relations is inadequate, in that it fails to establish in the Negro child a feeling of personal adequacy in meeting situations. Apparently no dependable directives growing out of strategic philosophies have been developed, in the family or elsewhere, which enable children to protect themselves from personality encroachments.

Responses of parents indicate that churches contribute little to the lives of their membership in the way of racial understanding. Interracial activities are practically nonexistent in low income groups, and are looked upon with suspicion by them. Upper income parents report more belief in the sincerity of these groups, but there is no evidence that their activities, which aim at bettering race relations, have any influence on parental guidance.

It appears from these data that color caste subjects the Negro child to interferences and limitations in relation to the attainment of full human acceptance and status; that such interference with social goals results in frustration; that the Negro child is therefore faced with emotional difficulties because of caste status and social controls. It further appears that guidance received lacks power, and that, as a result of the total impact, Negro children may be forced into adopting inadequate ego-defenses.

IMPLICATIONS

A practical application of the facts revealed by children themselves might be made to the training and guidance of the children. The needs of the Negro child are no different, of course, from those of any other children; but the chances of their being met may be less, for rewards in the larger world of which they are a part are few. Conscientious attempts on the part of individual majority members to eliminate in their behavior those manifestations which serve as instigators of ill-feeling would be a long step in reducing the odds prevailing.

Intercultural education groups might consider these specifics pointed out by children as annoying, and use the facts revealed as a basis for a constructive, active program. Well-meaning individuals may be ignorant of factors, in their own behavior, which have negative influences. Such ignorance may be dispelled through the dissemination of information, with the subsequent possibility of conscious modification of such behavior.

In passing, it should be noted that children mentioned of their own accord some experiences which were valued by them and which contributed to their social understanding. For example, one boy of the low income group in New York commented: "I had a nice white teacher last year. She let us have the Youth Builders Club. We had forums and learned about discrimination. When I was turned away from the movie theatre I knew why. It was because they don't let children in after a certain hour when they are by themselves. If a white boy my age had been there and they let him in and not let me in, then I would know why I didn't get in."

A girl of this group volunteered: "I went up to Columbia University once. I don't remember the floor. The teacher took us. We went to hear a doctor speak. There were some children there. They were white children. We had to wait a while for the doctor, but when she came, she told us about different people, and she said that the color of your skin didn't make any difference. That made me feel pretty good. They asked a lot of questions and they said we had to get along together. It is all right to marry someone not your color if you can get along with them. When she got through talking, the children talked to each other, and all of us laughed and had a good time."

Another child commented: "I went to a summer school at 129th and Amsterdam Avenue. That was a fine school. They had all kinds of shops and a roof gym. They served a fine menu. There were plenty of white children there, and they didn't seem to mind the colored children. We all played together and had a swell time."

A boy stated: "There was a white teacher who helped us with plays. We gave one play at the Service Center. A white boy was the bum. I was the main character."

All of these unsolicited statements throw some light on the kinds of techniques which have already been successfully used by white persons in their attempts at bettering human relationships. Perhaps much help and understanding is gained from direct verbal approaches by competent adults. Experiences which include first-hand contact with white children under wise guidance would also seem to make meaningful contributions. As pointed out earlier, however, mere proximity is not in itself an ameliorating factor.

Though society offers evidence of some improvement in the area under consideration, certainly much yet remains to be done. Social reforms are slow. The most economical arrangement from the point of view of time is to make the best possible adjustment in the culture in which one is born and probably will die but at the same time to strive toward a more compatible one. The preceding account gives some insight into the kinds of anxieties mobilized by our society and inherent in the social milieu. Of importance is consideration of the possibilities of defense which can be offered.

It is apparent that the Negro child needs an enriched program of training which places more emphasis on the building of attitudes toward himself—attitudes especially of self-esteem, self-respect, and self-confidence. The isolation of existing pressures and notation of the feelings accompanying them, as in this study, might serve as the basis for the development of specific survival techniques or adjustment mechanisms to offset the effects of the difficulties.

The urgency of the need for parent education, a relatively neglected area among Negroes, is apparent. At present, these children can turn to no source for adequate help. Negroes themselves have a great responsibility in attending more seriously to the complete growth of children of their group. They might also consider educating each other toward making some initial approaches in friendly intergroup relations.

LIMITATIONS OF THE STUDY

One factor not covered in this study is that of the general adjustment of the children interviewed. How often do they have trouble regardless of the racial identity of the others involved? Some individuals may have trouble regardless of the setting. Personalities of this kind were not identified in the study.

A second consideration not explored is concerned with the effect of hostile impulses aroused in intercultural conflicts on intracultural relations. There is a possibility that such hostility, which finds no legitimate outlet, is projected within the group, presenting itself in a form of misplaced aggression.

A study of these two factors would contribute much to a further understanding of some aspects of human behavior.

BIBLIOGRAPHY

Criswell, Joan. *A Sociometric Study of Race Cleavage in the Classroom.* Archives of Psychology, No. 235. New York, Columbia University, 1939. 82 p.

Davis, Allison and Dollard, John. *Children of Bondage.* Washington, D. C., American Council on Education, 1940. 299 p.

Dollard, John, and others. *Frustration and Aggression.* New Haven, Yale University Press, 1939. 209 p.

Graphic Facts About St. Louis and St. Louis County. St. Louis Social Planning Council, 1947.

Johnson, Charles S. *Patterns of Negro Segregation.* New York, Harper and Brothers, 1943. 332 p.

Odum, Howard and Moore, Harry Estill. *American Regionalism.* New York, Henry Holt and Company, 1938. 693 p.

Shaffer, Laurance F. *The Psychology of Adjustment.* Boston, Houghton Mifflin Company, 1936. 600 p.

Warner, William Lloyd, and others. *Color and Human Nature.* Washington, D. C., American Council on Education. 1941. 301 p.

APPENDIX A

INTERVIEW FORM FOR CHILDREN

Place where interview took place ....

Name .... Age .... Sex ....

Place of birth ....

Length of time in New York ....

Present address ....

Previous address ....

Length of time at present address ....

Name of Mother ....

Name of Father ....

Occupation: Mother ....

           Father ....

Church or Sunday School attendance ....

Record:

INTERVIEW QUESTIONS FOR CHILDREN

I. Have you some good friends here at school? What is it that you like about them? Are any of these white children? Who is your best friend? Is he (or she) white or colored? Do you play with white children very much? Tell me about it.

II. Do you ever have misunderstandings or quarrels or fights with other children? Are there some children who seem to want to fight more than others? Which children are they? Are these colored children or white children, or are they both white and colored? Do some children at your school do things which you do not like? What do they do? Tell me what happens. Are these things ever done by white children? When this happened (name specific item mentioned) how did you feel? What did you feel like doing? What did you do? Did it work? Did you tell your mother? What did she say? Did you do it? Did it work? Do colored children do these things too? How do you feel? What do you do?

III. Have white children ever made fun of you? What did they say? When this happened how did you feel? What did you feel like doing? What did you do? Did you tell your mother about it? What did she tell you to do? Since then have you done what your mother told you to do? (Why? or Why not?) Do colored children ever make fun of you? What do they say? How do you feel? What do you do? Does it work?

IV. Do you have a white teacher or a colored teacher? Is she nice to the class? Is she nice to you? Does she like colored children? Why do you say what you do? Whom does she like best in the class? Is this a colored child? What do you want to be when you grow up? Have you told your teacher about it? What does she say about it? Do you think that she would like for you to become a doctor, lawyer, or teacher? Does your room ever have class plays, entertainments, or programs? Have you ever taken part in one? Tell me about the part which you had. How did you come to get it? Did you choose it? How did you feel about the part? Did you like it? (If part was not liked): What did you do about it? What did your mother say about it? Does the class ever take trips away from school? Do you have a good time with the white children on the trips?

V. Do you ever have trouble with the grocer, butcher, bakery shop man, or candy store man? Tell me about it. Do you ever have to wait long in order to be served? Why do you think this happens? How do you feel when these things happen? What do you feel like doing? What do you do? What does your mother say you should do?

VI. Have you ever been turned away from a park, playground, museum, or any place where other people go? What happened? How did you feel? What did you feel like doing? What did you do? Did you tell your mother? What did she say?

VII. Do you go to the movies? What do you think about movies with Negro characters? Do you like them? Do you listen to the radio? What do you think about Negro radio characters? Do you like them?

VIII. Have you ever gone into an all-white neighborhood? How did you feel? What happened? (If interracial experience is reported): What did you do? Did you tell your mother? What did she say about it?

IX. Do you go to Sunday school? Does your Sunday school teacher tell you to try to get along with white people? What does she say?

X. What does your mother say to you about getting along with white people?

APPENDIX B

INTERVIEW FORM FOR PARENTS

Parent's name ....
Address ....
Occupation ....
   Length of time in present employment ....
Place of birth ....
   Length of time in present city ....
Skin coloring ....
Church attendance ....
Interracial activities ....

INTERVIEW QUESTIONS FOR PARENTS

    I. Have your children ever reported to you any experiences which they have had with white children or white adults? Do your children willingly report these experiences or do you have to elicit them?

   II. What were some of these experiences? How did you handle the situation? Did your suggestion help? Why do you think so? Is your child obedient? Does he take your advice or is he inclined to do what he chooses?

  III. How would you handle each of the following situations? What do you think is the best advice to give your child in each situation? If he is called nigger, sambo, snowball, or any other such name? If he is told that he must play a slave or servant role in a play? If white children fight him? If he is turned away from a park, playground, museum, theatre, or any place where other people go?

  IV. Do you often come in contact with white people? Do you have any white friends? Do you exchange visits? How often do you visit with white friends?

   V. Do you belong to any interracial groups? Do you get help from them? What good do you think they serve?

  VI. Do you think white people are justified in demanding a degree of segregation?

 VII. What is your minister's attitude on Negro–white relations? What does he tell you to do when racial situations arise? What is his advice? Is he a fair-minded person? Do you think of him as a peacemaker?

VIII. What do you think is the greatest need in Negro–white relations?